M000235732

Stay
Young
To
100

Charlotte Hackin

To Kim + Shannon

Enjoy!

Charlotte Hackin

Published by GLOBE PRESS

Copyright © 2015 by Charlotte Hackin

All rights reserved under International and Pan American copyright Conventions. No Part of this book may be reproduced or transmitted in any form or by any means, electronic or mechanical, photocopying, recording, or by any information storage and retrieval system, without the written permission of the publisher.

Library of Congress Cataloging In Publication Data

ISBN 978-1879081093

2008937336

Printed in the United States of America

GLOBE PRESS LOS ANGELES

DEDICATED

To my beloved husband Sam, my rock who encouraged me all through my many creative years.

To my three sons Steven, Dennis and Carey, and grandson Danny.

CONTENTS

ACKNOWLEDGMENTS

I've been fortunate in my life time to know personally and work with many professional people, skilled in their particular field, provided knowledge and direction needed in writing this book. Before one sentence took shape, my research disclosed invaluable secrets, to live a healthy lifestyle with a message for all ages to benefit.

Many thanks to my dear friend, Linda Niemiec, Vice President of Development for Crusader Clinic, a healthcare service for families in Rockford. Her keen input and direction called attention to various topics, and helped channel important subjects which I incorporated. Her knowledge has proven invaluable.

I would like to express my thanks to Wanda Hoover, an LCPC, a license Clinical Professional Counselor, for her many suggestions regarding constructive approaches to troubled children and adults in family relationships.

I owe a special debt of gratitude to Carol Child, PHD, Masters in Social Studies, Masters in Social Work, and Clinical Social Worker for her many ideas, support, and knowledge during the time spent on the manuscript.

The book wouldn't be complete if I didn't mention a very special person, Webbs Norman, Emeritus Executive Director of the Rockford Park District of Illinois, for his guidance what is essential to the quality of life, enjoying nature, helping one to stay healthy, and well being.

ACKNOWLEDGEMENTS

A special thanks to Patrick Goeckner, a Financial Advisor, who made me realize the importance of conducting proper money management in personal and family matters.

I appreciate Stanley Campbell, executive director of Rockford Urban Ministries, who was insightful with his contribution on spirituality.

Jodell Lofgren, Certified Massage Therapist, brought to light the importance of massage helping one to relax, and reduce tension.

I am deeply grateful to Sue Cichock, for generously assisting in editing the final draft.

A great debt of thanks is owed to the hundreds of researchers, scholars, and journalists without the input, whose work this book would not have come about.

The Front Cover was designed by Graphic Designer, Kari Holzinger.

INTRODUCTION

I was brought into this world with the help of my father, a doctor along with my grandmother, a well known midwife. I was blessed. How many can attest to having such a birth?

I have seen the papers and know they filled out my birth certificate: In the State of Illinois—City of Chicago, all names and particulars are there and recorded.

Whenever someone brings up age, they hedge around wanting to know just how old I am. I grin and shake my head. "I'm flattered— keep going! Keep going!" Their eyes open wide surprised. I don't feel my age, nor do I look it.

I have often felt that my parents made a mistake on my birth certificate. I'm 90 years young. My grandmother lived to be 104. Since I think positive, eat healthy, exercise everyday, and keep the right attitude, I have good reason to believe that I'll meet her goal.

Everyone assumes one is wiser with age. I know plenty of educated people in their prime, who are half my age and aren't living very wise lives. They might eat healthy and exercise, but they think negatively and aren't too happy. Their life cups are always half empty, whereas my life cup is always filled.

I heard members of the family mentioning how old Granny was, still going strong past 100. I loved being with my grandmother. I remember asking, *what were her secrets for a long life?* She smiled and said, "if I had the secret I'd be a millionaire: Eat healthy foods, a little wine doesn't hurt, and never carry bad thoughts about another person, because it makes you unhappy. You have to have a reason, a purpose that makes the living worthwhile each day. No matter how long you live, it's easier just to stay positive— you'll live to be 100." Then she hugged me.

I have had my share many misfortunes in life, for example, my oldest sister had a nervous breakdown when in her teens. It was also sad to witness my parent's divorce after twenty-five years of marriage, and observing how they handled their unfortunate, unhappy situation, with an ill child. There were lessons learned in patience, empathy, tolerance and understanding of the human mind. I matured early and had deep insight understanding human emotions. I tried to remember how my granny spoke often about staying positive.

For me, the worst was when my youngest son, Carey, at just sixteen was killed by a drunk driver. With the sudden death of our son, our lives completely changed overnight. It is shocking to one's state of mind. If someone has a long, slow illness it is one thing, but your child in his prime of life, taken from you in one brief second, saying goodnight and the next day gone. Shocking! Frightening!

With that horrific time in my life, I wondered if would I ever find new meaning, or new strength for a new day. Would I ever find something to smile about?

Life's experiences can tear you apart. The suddenness of Carey's tragic death was shattering. The months following, were a blur of grief. Those frightening days left me depleted, empty, forsaken, and wanting. My spirit was shattered.

Fighting all my demons kept dragging me emotionally down, it was the lowest point in my life. I was popping tranquilizers, downing them with alcohol, and trying to dull my senses, praying to drive the pain mixed with anger away— "why him?"

The most regrettable thing was that my husband, my pillar of strength, who I turned to, was no better off than I. Once we were two people who loved, now we were distant. I walked around a sad soul, lost in grief. Months went by while I experienced days of gloom, and never wanting to leave my bed. I found little reason for life.

One morning while applying my make-up with a trembling hand, staring back in the mirror at my haggard face, I burst out crying uncontrollably, and I knew right then I had to change— my mental pictures were all wrong. I was destroying myself emotionally and physically. I was mentally drained.

I learned you can't run away from trouble. If you want to live without trouble, die young before anything negative happens.

Change for me had to happen—today, right now!

CHAPTER 1

What I Overcame

"Courage is very important. Like a muscle, it is strengthened by use."

Ruth Gordon

One word that entered deep in my brain and that I hung onto was the word— "SHOULD."

I **should stop!** Taking tranquilizers....
I **should stop!** Drinking....
I **should stop!** This mental downgrade....
It was time to accept **that** my self destructive life wasn't bringing my son back. I was no good to myself, to his memory, or to my family. More positive constructive thoughts were the beginning:

Thinking positive! Brings positive results....
Thinking positive! Brings happiness....
Thinking positive! One begins to live....
Thinking positive! One is free of stress....
Time is a healer. It gives us the strength to find ways to overcome hardship and build confidence again.
Life is like a mirror if we frown at it, it frowns back.

WHAT I OVERCAME

If we smile, it returns the greeting. I learned that the hard way. One secret is to get busy the instant a wrong mental picture occurs, and push it out of your consciousness. Doing so will change what you think and do, and help you overcome any negative thoughts. There is power in understanding the thought process.

The only positive thing about trouble is that all of us encounter it in our lives, some more than others. We share a bond— a oneness— a knowing experience. We can feel each other's pain.

The best way to get your mind off your own troubles is to try to help someone else with his. I found this from my own experience.

"When I dig another out of trouble, the hole from which I lift him is the place where I bury my own."

Chinese proverb

Most people yearn to know their purpose in life. We come into this life without anything, and leave it with nothing. We can't take our achievements with us. So you have to ask questions to make your days more meaningful—happier.

The beauty of the spirit is what we feel the most in our youth. It is something that we should hold onto. When young, we know no fear. Along the way, with a couple of knocks our confidence lessens.

Only you alone are in control. Only you and you alone can choose to set your mind where you want to be, when the unexpected happens. You may not be able to stop the unexpected, but with effort you can choose the state of mind you want to be.

One has a choice— to stay negative on the verge of cycling down, or positive— clear headed, one's higher self, enjoying life more.

I made my choice: "Clear your mind and the rest will follow." I listened to my inner-voice and focused my thoughts on the word "Should."

Dr. Herbert Benson came up with a study about the mind which holds truth about how obsessing over worries leads to stress, which holds us back and clouds judgment. Stepping away from problems, backing off from them, makes handling those problems easier and clearer.

Pick up on a hobby; it helps to divert your thoughts. Go plant a garden in which you can sit when you're digging days are done, and year after year it will bloom and ripen. Hours spent relaxing in the garden will pay off.

Gardening relieves stress. Working the soil, being outdoors, and touching the plants all relieve tension. Bending down and pulling weeds is good as weight lifting. Pushing a lawn mower has the same beneficial effect on bone density as weight training does. Besides gardening, take the dog for a walk. If you focus on making and doing something, your mind is distracted.

Biking is great fun for the entire family. The attached child trailer to the back of your bike enables you to include your youngster and enjoy the day.

The Japanese did research on hobbies. Out of 1200 people studied, they found that men who engage in hobbies are less likely to come down with circulatory disorders than those who don't. Mind boosting activities, challenge the brain and, keeps you healthier, and also keeps you from growing old sooner.

There is an achievement in finding the "art in living" and getting sixty minutes from the twenty-four hours of the day or better yet, adding life to your years. Hobbies reduce stress. Studies show hobbies strengthen your immunity. Have you ever thought of enrolling in a painting class? Try it before you die. It's fun if you have not done so.

A centenarian, famous Russian artist Moses Fesigin, was still painting at the age of 103. The whole world is open, you won't have time to dwell on anything, but giving your full attention to that creative moment, you become distracted from everyday problems. Your entire being is absorbed in the planning of your picture: what colors, what paint, getting it down. You need your hands to do something other than wipe your teary eyes. There is nothing that distracts so completely as seeing the colors and design take shape on your canvas. There is no room for negative thoughts in your mind.

People engaged in hobbies are less likely to suffer mental decline. Many of them are socially involved people with the same likes. By being involved with interests and the world around you, your days are easier to cope with.

Frank Calloway, another artist who at 112 years old is still painting visions of his youth into murals. I would be remiss if I didn't mention York Garrett, III, a black man who overcome many hardships in 101 years, and got into Howard University's pharmacy school, served in 1916 in World War l, and returned to graduate from Howard with honors. After which, he opened his own drugstore.

Descartes is famous for his saying, "I think therefore I am." He believed the mind was always at work, even in sleep. One thing that he believed was, some public praise is good for your ego. It also could extend your life. Something as small as winning praise, perhaps from a job well done, will not only boost your ego, but add well-being.

It is hard to believe, but studies have been made about winning the Oscar. Actors who win live nearly four years longer than the actors who never get nominated. The logic behind this suggests being liked and appreciated confers health benefits. It boosts your ego, making you feel good—important. Your blood pressure will be normal and you are at peace—calm.

If painting pictures isn't your thing, perhaps try volunteering at a hospital, where seeing your smile brings someone much pleasure for a tiny moment.

You might not get a statue, but in your mind it will make you feel very good to be doing something worthwhile, and you will be preoccupied with things other then thinking about yourself. One good positive action, in the right direction is all it takes!

Listen to your inner-voice speak. "I will think positive not negative." Repeat out loud: "I and only I have the power within myself to make a change, by doing so I will take my worries and fears and make them vanish." Wipe that frown off your face. Stand before a mirror — smile! Laugh! Think of something pleasant— a lovers kiss— a small compliment that pleased you. It is one step, that helps you keep mentally balanced and less stressed. It will help you will reap the rewards and stay young to 100.

WHAT I OVERCAME

CHAPTER 2

Laughter is Therapeutic

Bob Hope lived to be 100. "I have seen what a laugh can do. It can transform almost unbearable tears into something bearable, even hopeful."

Bob Hope

Many of us take life too seriously, letting small things disturb us. We all need a sense of humor in these times. I've known a few people who unconsciously spoil their lives and the lives of those around them.

Laughter is very therapeutic. Laughter heals. Being able to laugh, see some kind of humor in difficult situations can help. You stay healthy; it may be a buffer against heart attacks. Laughter protects against stress. Perhaps regular laughter should be on the list of each day, along with finding humor. Laugh those sad thoughts away. Strange how the mind works, if we think that this too shall pass— so it does.

"Laughter is an instant vacation."   **Milton Berle**

LAUGHTER IS THERAPEUTIC

George Burns the comedian lived to be 100. "I have a great set of genes, a great sense of humor and a great capacity to never give up working and loving."

"I'm always relieved when someone delivers a eulogy and I realize I'm listening to it."

George Carlin

At Loma Linda University in California, studies were done on laughter and medical benefits. In the years past several scientists tried to uncover and understand the physiology of laughter. More work is needed, but the studies are encouraging.

One thing scientists are doing is working with MRI machines, placing people in them and making them laugh, to study what happens to the brain. They found out humor stimulates parts of the brain that send out dopamine, which makes you feel good. Laughter is addictive to the brain, that dopamine - you want to do more of it.

"A merry heart doeth good like a medicine."

Anonymous

When we laugh, we use as many as 15 small muscles which squeeze our faces, helping it to smile. If the laugh is hearty enough, and almost takes our breath away, tears will begin to flow from our tear ducts.

Further studies found that laughter affects every part of the body, like the inner lining of the blood vessels,

12

which produce good chemicals when the blood vessels expand, and bad chemicals when they contract.

The tests performed were simple enough. A pressure cuff was placed on the subject's wrist, and pumped to restrict blood flow. During that brief time, the person watched a scene from a funny movie.

The doctor then used another machine to see whether the blood vessel lining expanded or contracted. It expanded during the funny clip, giving off good chemicals, which has the ability to reduce clotting and inflammation. The benefits are extensive, so try keeping your spirits high and finding some humorous saying to giggle, now that you know the positive results.

After watching a sad scene, the vessels gave off stress hormones. Unfortunately, many reaching their golden years find less to smile about. One reason they leave living behind is the idea that the opportunity to do something that will keep them in the main stream and active in living, has passed them by. If ailing it is understandable, but many feel this way because they have put very little effort into living. These people are inexcusable. Perhaps you know of such a person, it might even be a member of the family. Getting them interested in once again becoming a member of the human race is a worthy attempt.

Humor helps us to balance to our lives. The ability to make light of a situation detaches us for the moment from what troubles us and clears our inner mind. Like a door opening, our mind will then suggest a way out. We can't solve anything too close to whatever is troubling us.

Humor your mind. Keep your cool when tied up in traffic. Perhaps there's been an accident, making cars move at a snail's pace. You sit and slowly get more stressed because you have to be at the office right now!

You sit in your car pulling your hair out, thinking, "I can run faster than this car is moving!" You can bang on your wheel and cuss, or you can ask yourself if can you do anything about this uncomfortable situation. Try diverting your mind, thinking of something pleasant, or humorous.

Everything in life is motion. It's like the tides...you can't hold it back— it's moving and changing —it's progress. I've said it before, life owes us nothing, we owe it everything! Don't pigeon-hole yourself. Give to some sort of charity, you will feel worthwhile. When you feel unsure, get into a slump, find a purpose. Direct your thoughts, "away from yourself!"

What does one's positive thoughts, along with diet, exercise, and a healthy way of life, have to do with staying and looking younger for longer? Think of the reverse and the consequences. Aren't these conclusions reasonable to think and act upon them?

Because man is such a complicated being, and is born with both what he inherits along with his environment; it is what an individual goes through, leaves its mark throughout their lives. Each experience shapes who we are. At some moments during the difficult times, it isn't easy to keep reinforcing one's mind, to stay calm, to find a positive attitude to hold onto, and to keep mind over matter.

"Attitude" is everything, it impacts every part of life. It makes the journey that much easier, if we don't lose sight of the fact that "attitude" is a major key for staying positive. We have a choice every day regarding the opinion we embrace for that day.

"Your Attitude," is more important than failures, than successes, than what other people think or say or do. We cannot change the inevitable. I learned that! The only thing we can do is play on the one thing that we have, and that is our feelings.

Everyone, by the time they reach maturity, should have some control over their own destiny. It helps to have a proper attitude. How we think changes everything and impacts our lives.

Attitude sustains us. All of us have a choice every day regarding the attitude we take. What people say or do is 90% how we react to it. I repeat, we have choice in what attitude we decide to hold onto—good days will happen!

"You are a child of the universe...nurture strength of spirit to shield you in sudden misfortune...strive to be happy, do not feign affection, neither be cynical about love; for in the face of all aridity and disenchantment it is perennial as the grass."

Desiderata

Strive to be happy. Isn't this what you want out of your days? It takes mind over matter... most of the time, it really doesn't matter. To help achieve this ultimate good feeling, make a decision to set new patterns of thought, to help carry you along one day at a time.

CHAPTER 3

Stopping Stress

"Enjoy the day! It is yours for the making."

Anonymous

Stress works on the entire nervous system, causing a chemical change; and the creation of toxic poisons which reacts destructively upon the body. We feel and start to look, tired and old. Those worried creases on our brow become deeper.

Focus on what Desiderata said, especially when you are going through hard times, we all need the arm of a warm embrace...we are needy!

When I was going through the grief of losing of my son, I became physically ill. My blood pressure was dangerously, high. That's what stress, tension, and unhappiness will do to your mind and body.

Your mind can't reason or make proper decisions. Optimistic thought stimulates these same nerve centers, and brings about a healthy chemical zing in your body. Your health, and staying and looking younger than your years are influenced by your mind:

STOPPING STRESS

"Age is not a matter of years; it is a matter of outlook."

Anonymous

Your outlook is written on your face! If the image that comes before you is negative, that thought picture which we can refer to as the resourceful mind, is problem solving. If your picture thoughts are negative, only you can stop them. Only you can feed good images into your mind. Sometimes it's difficult, but the rewards make you feel good— and look good.

Your unconscious **resourceful mind** thinks, you want this to occur— it is mind over matter and it obeys what you think. It is a slow process of rethinking but it will make for good images.

Grandma Moses was a recognized painter, who did her first painting at 85. She went through some trying times raising four children. One year the children came down with scarlet fever, when asked about it later, all she could say was, "that was a very hard year! It passed on like all the rest."

She could describe in loving and small detail her wedding dress, or a holiday dinner, but something about that hard year, she brushed aside, and found nothing worth to remember except that she would comment, "it passed on like all the rest!"

One reason why she remained alert, vigorous, and lively in her nineties, was because she had a philosophy:

STAY YOUNG TO 100

"To remember the beauty, the laughter, and for all the disappointments, the hardship, the unhappy moments, let it pass."

Grandma Moses

She didn't dwell upon bad things! How right was she? If we can block the hard times, the disappointments, and the anger from our lives, it can be lived longer, and younger.

According to one of the largest studies ever done on 100 year olds, the four most important things you can do in your quest to live younger and longer are: Lighten your emotional load. Eat and drink in moderation. Consciously challenge your brain. Stay in touch with your old friends and make new ones.

If you shed stress, it adds years to your life. Stress comes in many disguises—backaches, headaches. It might even be a grown married child going through trying times that we find stressful.

Anxiety and tension are part of life's experience. Each of us can learn to accept and turn our minds outward, enabling us to handle life better and enjoy it to the fullest.

Your inner spirit and thinking positive brings you closer to feeling worthwhile, it also keeps you void of anger, resentments; and strengthens your thoughts and to help you welcome a better new day.

"There is an art to living."

Henry Thoreau

Henry Thoreau said to affect the quality of life is the highest art. I can attest to it. I have kept a positive image and still young in spirit. I watch what I eat. I am busy still exhibiting my art. I write and am actively engaged in the main stream of life. I keep busy doing, not sitting around rusting, and watching life pass me by.

I am one of the Commissioners in an elected, six year term for the Rockford, Illinois Park District, when it ends, I plan to run again. Staying involved gives one a sense of control of over life and something to contribute to society. I know from firsthand experience that the true joy in life is being used for a purpose, being thoroughly worn out.

No one who lives only for himself can be happy. The genuine pleasures and the excitement of living comes from immersion in something, anything that we know to be bigger, better, more enduring, and worthier than we are.

People, ideas, and causes offer the one possible escape not merely from selfishness, but from the hungers of solitude and the sorrows of aimlessness.

No person is as uninteresting as a person without interests. The pitiful people are those who, in their living elect to be spectators rather than participants; the tragic ones are those sightseers who turn their back deliberately on the procession.

Experience all that life has to offer, don't just be a spectator. Learn to be pleased with yourself. Keep a positive image; believe that you have become wiser with age. Talk to yourself. Let yourself know you're doing the best you can. Age is not a matter of years, realize that your mind is an electronic instrument; it is your whole physical body. Your health is definitely influenced by your mind.

Look inside yourself and you will be surprised how many out-of-date ideas and wrong reactions to things you have pushed out of sight, and have almost forgotten, that clutter up your powers for clear thinking. They influence your reactions, which keep you from moving ahead. See yourself starting each new day with a clean positive slate.

Don't permit your subconscious mind to take over. Your subconscious mind is a powerful force. You can use it to help yourself. It does what your conscious mind tells it to do. Once you tell your subconscious mind what to do, it slowly finds its way until it reaches a conclusion and solves your problem. Your stress factor will lessen.

For a city gal, living on a ranch was an new experience for me. Every day was exciting and scary with many unknown elements. By the second year my husband realized that having a dairy and getting up at the crack of dawn to milk three times a day, seven day a week, wasn't what we wanted. I surely felt better when we changed over to feeding beef cattle. It was a different operation. All that was needed was laying the feed in the troughs, to get the cattle fat for market. The transfer was costly, as troughs and overhead shelters had to be built, plus other physical structures arranged to accommodate this feeding operation.

Our neighbors fed cattle, and we all bought cotton meal and grain from the Mill in the area. Unknown to us, all the cattle feeders were being ripped off by the Mill owner, who extracted the oil from the seed, selling Cotton Meal. We were feeding three hundred head of cattle little more than ground up hulls, which had little nourishment.

As the months went by, we kept pouring more feed into the cattle, spending more money without results. Normally cattle should gain weight in 90 days, and be ready to be shipped to market. Our financial loss was great. It was a very difficult period for us.

It's the moments in my life, not the days, that stick in my mind. During this very trying period, on the cattle ranch I did all I could to find emotional strength, and give my husband support he needed. I couldn't help being angry when I thought about the Mill ripping off and stealing from all the ranchers, financially ruining many. It wasn't easy hiding our worries and fears from the children, who sensed our daily tension. It was a frightening time, our money was dangerously low.

Each person reacts differently to stress. For me, it was tension headaches. For my husband, it was backaches and chain smoking.

Stress goes hand in hand with various sorts of ailments. Often times we never relate to the stress factor to what brings it on. Stress affects the body sooner or later. It challenges all one's internal systems. It weakens the immune system. It makes us old in spirit and old in how we act and look.

Throughout one's life there will be defining moments. Some can be big disappointments. Be aware how you react and find ways to find courage. If it's just a stupid blunders everyone makes, do your best to forget about it as soon as possible and move on. It's during those difficult, defining moments that one can really discover what they are made of.

During those daunting times, I worked hard to stand beside my husband, which made the fight less difficult for both of us. I made a conscious decision to stop exploding about things that for the moment couldn't be changed, and tried to think calmly, instead of thinking negatively, and I pitched in where I was needed.

My husband took on the fight with the other ranchers to see that justice prevailed. Finally, after almost a year, the owner of the Mill made good. He knew better than to confront two hundred ranchers who threatened to bring a lawsuit, and something far worse.

That year wasn't a good one. Like Grandma Moses, I put it aside, and only concentrated on all the better ones. There was much to be thankful for.

Emerson wrote…

"Finish every day and be done with it. You have done what you could. Tomorrow is a new day; begin it well, this day is all that is good and fair. It is too dear with its hopes and invitation, to waste a moment on yesterdays."

These are truths to carry out in your thought process. Each of us wants to be happy, but how we go about it is another thing. It takes effort to clear your subconscious mind of wrong mental pictures. You cannot afford to let your past mistakes or past hurts cloud your future. It stops you from making good decisions and moving ahead. Visualize a happy mental image, only you can make it all happen. It is within your power with the right thinking.

Try and reject obstacles by making a list of the problems that you would like to eliminate from your life. Don't concentrate on just the small ones. Schedule some time to set aside so you can fix these problems. You can begin with the easiest to solve. Setbacks come to everyone.

STOPPING STRESS

Charles F. Kettering, the great inventive genius, remarked, "I am not interested in the past. I am interested only in the future, for that is where I expect to spend the rest of my life." That future is where you are to spend the rest of your life; and it is determined by your outlook. You'll find all the resources for it in your mind. In these difficult times, it is more important than ever to reflect on what really matters. To think in simple ideals and seek to live a fuller, richer life.

Adversity can be turned around if you do something positive about it. Your thoughts can show you a way. Your future is determined by the proper mental attitude, of which you have complete control, if you desire it. Reflect on the word —"courage." Many of us go through our days with our recuperative powers impaired, so that minor hurts to the ego will not properly heal. Those who stage a comeback have one common characteristic, and that is, "emotional elasticity." People who have emotional elasticity bounce back fast, which is a sign of healthy functioning.

Emotional elasticity is the strength of mind to be able to brush aside lingering resentments, so that you can move on with your life. It is using a proper attitude for any given situation. Having emotional elasticity gives you a lot of flexibility, so that you don't snap like a rubber band and break. I repeat, it is thinking with good reasoning that helps us maintain healthy actions.

CHAPTER 4

Giving Up Resentment

"Anger, if not restrained, is more hurtful to us than the injury that provokes it."

Seneca

"Giving up resentments" is another step moving ahead. Sure you have a right to be angry, depressed, or resentful if you have been mistreated, whether by a member of the family, or at your job. But, when resentful, you turn over control of your emotional life to others.

We all, at one time or another, have met that bitter person, who never let go of a hurt, or a personal disappointment. They nurse grudges, and can't enjoy life, or those around them. Nothing is more damaging to one's health and appearance than holding on to the hurts in life.

People are often lonely, and alone because of their grumpy moods, pushing away the very people they want near. Think about it! If you are caught up with getting even at someone who might have done something to you, in the end, revenge is never sweet. It can almost destroy you. If you train your mind, it will think and send signals to your subconscious letting it know, you're thinking negative. If you take control, and reverse mental pictures that work against you, and pull you down mentally and physically, you can change your outlook and trigger an inner spark in your over all appearance and well being.

"If you're going to pursue revenge, you'd better dig two graves."

Chinese proverb

Dr. Thomas Peris, longevity expert, said: "if you tend to dwell on problems and internalize stress, it will take five years off your life." Make the effort not to dwell on the negative parts of your life, and you can add five years to it.

You can train yourself to rethink your problem and find a solution that will make a wrong a into a right. Realize how far to take it, for in the thinking process, something happens to you. As Dr. Peris says, "If you can fix it then do so. If not, back away and chalk it up as another experience to learn from."

It isn't easy; I speak from experience. When my husband trusted a close friend, and went into a business together without signing a contract. The trust was one sided, and my husband got cheated. It ate at him, nearly destroying him emotionally. His days were spent thinking of revenge. Eventually, he chalked it up to a bitter lesson learned. As Dr. Peris says, "If you can fix it than do so, if not, back away."

"Life owes us little, we owe it everything."

"Resentment is like drinking poison and waiting for it to kill your enemy." Resentment, anger, and worry, can drain your energy and will bring on anxiety. It never is productive, for every moment spent worrying, is a moment that cheats you out of time for better things. Positive thoughts help us stay young while growing old.

Don't put your happiness on hold. Live each day as if it was the last—enjoy yourself! What a grand, uplifting feeling. Don't throw it away with sad thoughts, remember that gem of a word— SHOULD!

Do you remember Martha Stewart? She was held on trial and going to jail, and served a sentence, When out being interviewed she was asked, "how did you manage while locked away in jail?" She replied, "I'm an optimistic person, taking a positive view of future outcome. I don't let myself get down." Don't let myself get down? She became master over her mind.

Her resourceful mind didn't permit her to think negative. Even in jail she kept busy, creatively trying to be what she always was — a teacher, showing the other inmates how to do things, spreading her hard earned knowledge, and staying busy. She was, and is a positive thinker; which makes her what she is today, still productive, looking better than ever, and not defeated.

"I am an optimist. It doesn't seem too much use being anything else."

Winston Churchill

One Sunday morning I happened to catch the young Preacher Joel Osteen, on television giving a sermon of hope and inspiration. What stuck in my mind was how he viewed coping with life's problems, and almost to the word, General Colin Powell quoted a similar impression.

Powell remarked, "In your car you have a big windshield and a tiny rear view mirror... there is nothing to look behind, but what's ahead!"

"There is nothing I can do what's in the rear-view mirror." He made reference to a few mistakes during the handling about Iraq having weapons of mass destruction. He implied that he doesn't look back in the small rear view mirror, but forward into the big windshield.

Worry never fixes anything! It is really a waste of time. Most of the time we put too much importance where it really doesn't matter. Discard the word "can't", and replace it with "can." It helps us to accept.

Life is forever filled with challenges. Every day we're confronted with making decisions. Sometimes little ones, sometimes big. Sometimes they turn out negative, but we should hope for positive.

We call upon our life's experience, which tells us in the course we have learned from, and what motivates us to the respond, and what our choice will finally be.

There are a few choices in this world we have the power to help make. Happiness is one. Learning the keys to happiness is how we start to find ways to train our minds in positive thinking..

The unfortunate thing is we let good days slip by. If we spent the same amount of time being positive, as one might work staying negative, life would be lived with more wisdom, and a better attitude for making each day more fulfilling.

STAY YOUNG TO 100

"There is an art to living."

Harvard psychiatrist John Ratey provides much recent knowledge on brain research, which gives insight into why we think, feel and act the way we do. There are many ways we, can use this knowledge to improve our lives.

For one, we've learned how flexible the brain is. Once, we thought people were born with a set number of brain cells, and that we lose them as we age. Now we know that the brain keeps makes new cells every day.

This is good news. Our minds stay active, and positive change is possible at any age. Exercise improves mood by increasing levels of dopamine and serotonin. Physical exercise keeps the brain fit by increasing blood flow to the brain and promoting blood to the brain. Learning something different from what you do daily helps to train the brain for best response. Also, working crossword puzzles, and playing chess are good for the brain.

Pursue unfamiliar activities outside your routine, especially activities that involve movement, such as: tennis, skating, or ballroom dancing.

Oh, one more thing, you might try brushing your teeth using the other hand. I switch from my right to my left hand about once a week. It makes one think. You feel awkward, there's a lack of dexterity, and you will actually feel yourself concentrating more.

Another brain exercise; try to write your name using your other hand —that is a challenge. It too, takes powers of concentration. It looks like a four year old trying to write. These exercises are simple and not very time consuming, but the benefits are many.

GIVING UP RESENTMENT

When I was teaching art, one of the exercises was a **"tactile experience."** I had my student's draw their hand. There are steps, remember the word "tactile." Read these directions slowly and try it.

Sit down at the table with pencil and paper, your free hand resting in front of you. This is an important step: Begin looking at your thumb, which will be your starting point. *Never once do you look down at your paper while drawing. Your eyes will be looking at your fingers, moving simultaneously with your pencil concentrating on the subject.*

As your eyes move ever so slowly around the outer edges of your thumb, and slowly over each finger, move your pencil on the paper. Never permit your eyes to move faster than the hand with pencil. It is coordinating your eyes with the pencil. Work until you come around each finger, stopping when you reach the little finger. You will chuckle at the end results, which will appear crude—more like a child's work. The exercise helps you stay mentally lively. It is all part of the equation staying mentally healthy.

What we do to prevent looking and feeling old, not always is what we ingest, but how we manage daily problems mentally, and how we keep the stress factor to a minimum—looking younger longer.

Stress results in the body breaking down. Some people have pounding headaches. Stress challenges all of your organ systems and weakens your immune system. It may involve a troubled marriage, a job, a death, or grief. Each of us at some time will experience a host of everyday problems. Our immune system will weaken, we will get more colds, our energy level will go down.

CHAPTER 5

Be Money Wise

"An open mind collects more riches than an open purse."

Anonymous

Money problems seem to be what most families encounter. Stress can come about because of financial problems, which seem to increase during hard times. Trying to cope with financial problems, is hard on a marriage and can create distance between you and spouse. You need to think creatively, worry doesn't bring you closer to solving anything.

You shouldn't be the only one faced with the problem. It takes the co-operation of the entire family on unnecessary expenditures. Each member of your family should help, and each be part of your financial planning—getting them involved is important. Mapping out how their money is spent and what can they all do to live within a budget, will bring all of you closer to finding an answer.

Your own personal problems can't be solved by being in a state of worry. When your brain is "hot," you can't solve anything.

BE MONEY WISE

You need to sit down and think calmly. Mind over matter, is one suggestion that keeps you mentally strong, and helps with clearer problem solving. Money problems are major, and major steps are needed to correct them.

First, develop some kind of budget. It helps to keep a record of where and how the money is being spent. It is sometimes a chore, but it can be most helpful, alleviating anxiety at the end of the month when bills have to be met.

Sometimes it helps to lay out all your bills as you tally them by the month, make a plan of payment, and a plan to cut back spending. It is all there before you.

Lottery tickets and "get rich quick" schemes are something to look at when tallying weekly spending Before buying, think over. "it's only ten dollars!" but chasing the latest money-making opportunities can get expensive.

Develop a sound financial plan/ A practical money management plan helps you know where your money goes—few do. Change how you think about money, it makes a big difference. You need a practical approach to turn the problem around.

Questioning is important—do you really need another pair of new shoes when you bought a pair two months ago? Checks and balances are necessary for each adult member to track spending. It is very tempting when you see all those pretty things in the store. Stop and think, "Do I really need it— can I afford it?" Those handy credit cards take time to pay off. Keep only one; it makes it easier to pay each month. Pay off high-interest rate credit cards as quickly as possible.

If you feel down, does that mean you have to go shopping to get over your down mood? Spending unnecessarily, and living without a goal or a purpose will cause stress if you are not living within your means.

Try tracking your expenses carefully. If there is a need to have a second car, you can save money by leasing a used car. Stop and listen to that "inner-voice" that tells you you're doing the wrong thing. That whisper, or feeling, alerts you and knows you so well—if you listen to it, you will be buying less, and living within your means. That reinforcement will help you be less stressed.

In financial planning, while trimming expenses, you might think about cutting out that membership for you and partner at the gym, and starting exercise program at home. A jump rope, a large rubber ball, weights, and two legs to walk are all you need.

Entertainment, how many times do you all eat out? Eating in restaurants isn't cheap, even if you only eat at McDonalds. Think about cutting back on gifts to charities. Getting two rented movies for the price of going out to the movies is a savings. You're ahead already on making your own popcorn. Kick off your shoes, make yourself comfy and enjoy!

Whatever we are experiencing eventually shows up on our face. It is the first thing that we stare at. It reveals much. Financial problems bring on stress. Our face reflects our moods. In a way, it is a road map.

If you don't lose sight that, "mind over matter and attitude" are important keys, life's journey will be that much easier.

BE MONEY WISE

As long as we have the power to help ourselves, we are that much ahead. To sit back and think negative thoughts will not help. "Should" helps get us there! It calls attention to our negative thinking, which otherwise feeds on itself.

It's your subconscious mind that produces all ideas and solutions. The minute you relax, your subconscious mind makes things clear and slips the answer into you conscious mind.

It is said that Americans spend an average of $234 per person on holiday gifts. Before you spend, spend, spend, decide how much to spend on gifts this season and withdraw that amount from your bank. Put the money into separate envelopes with the name each person you are buying for. Bring those envelopes with you when shopping, and stop shopping when you have spent enough on the recipient that his or her envelope is empty. Boy, that's watching it. Think before spending. Your spouse or companion should be on the same page. If not, it becomes a major problem, especially when one wants to spend and the other wants to save.

This rule doesn't only apply during the holidays. Always watch where the money is going. Watch and keep in mind members in the family who are chronic spenders.

Consider a parental asset for purposes of federal financial aid—if the account is in the parent's name. This can help the student trying to get financial help, because colleges require students to use a greater percentage of their own assets to pay tuition and a lower percentage of their parents' assets. It is good to check directly with each college what their polices are.

With the price of gas sky high, start thinking in positive terms to help keep the budget in check. Drive the car no faster than sixty-five on the highway, where temptation to do eighty is utmost. Turn off the ignition when waiting for someone. Mind over matter can save you a dollar or two.

There is another rule to financial planning, and this to save for a "rainy day" to help you stay afloat in the event of a job loss. One good rule is to keep some cash reserve at your bank in a money market mutual fund. The reserve should be enough to cover three months' take-home pay. For safety, keep cash or travelers checks on hand to cover up to two weeks of expenses.

BE MONEY WISE

CHAPTER 6

Mental Serenity

"Relax the mind, it gives strength for tomorrows."

Pope

Yoga Younger Longer:

Taking time to clear your mind can boost your spirit and even help your immunity. Meditation first attracted scientific attention in the United States in the late 60s and early 70s when a Harvard Medical School cardiologist, Herbert Benson, began training heart patients in the technique. As their blood pressure and stress tests plummeted, the doctor became so impressed that he chronicled his finding in his book, "The Relaxing Response." It became a best seller. The number of people, in all walks of life, practicing meditation has grown.

Have you often thought that you never find time to pause and sit down to figure out what your life is all about? Our days are so full of things that must be done that taking time to just to sit quietly and do some abstract thinking doesn't seem to be in the cards.

MENTAL SERENITY

Studies were made by scientists at the University of Wisconsin. They gave 41 people a flu vaccine. A little more than half of the subjects learned to meditate and followed a regular schedule to meditate for one hour a day, six days a week.

The other group got the vaccine without meditating, and the scientists found that after eight weeks, mediators had higher levels of flu fighting antibodies than those who didn't meditate.

These 41 people were also better able to deal with stress. The studies showed that they sustained better moods with this feel-good effect lasting longer.

Researchers have been able to determine what effects these methods to relax have on our minds and bodies.

Meditation produces measurable, biological changes in the brain and body. Your every thought, word, and action causes a related chemical reaction. Meditation isn't difficult to practice, it doesn't require chanting or gazing or sitting in the lotus position. If you don't like where you're at, stop and find the other part of yourself which is calling out.

Some basics: Find fifteen minutes. It is a wonderful way to relax:

"Face yoga," Facial techniques are exercises that do wonders for keeping one looking younger. Here are a few suggestions for taking every part of the face and doing something with it:

The **"Eyes:"** shutting the eyes tight than relaxing still keeping them closed. Do this several times, than open, shut tight relax keep closed than open. The **"Eyes,"** help erase crow's-feet… Shift your eyes-darting in different directions.

The **"Tongue,"** stick your tongue way out—stretch it. Do this several times. If you feel a tingling sensation it is working.

The **"Cheeks,"** puffing your cheeks as if blowing on a horn will keep them supple.

***Breathing Meditation…** Find a quiet place, sit quietly and close your eyes.

***Begin** by slowly exhaling and inhaling as you normally do, gradually focus on your breathing, and the coming and going of your breath.

***Don't** let yourself wander, gradually return to your normal breathing, and focus on your breathing. The experience will begin to have positive effects on your stress level and your general state of mind.

To meditate is to go directly to the silent region within. Feel yourself ebbing, relaxing. It is hard to describe the feeling, but one thing is sure, you gain a new sense of being, a calming away of the daily strain—peace.

Detaching the mind from all outside activities is beneficial, many businessmen close their door at a certain time during the day. They sit in silence, shutting the outside world and freeing their mind so that there is nothing there. No sights, no sounds, cut it all off… don't talk to yourself for that produces thoughts, which produces images.

***Quiet consciousness…**This is difficult at first. Try detaching the mind from all activity. Make the time to sit for fifteen minutes alone. Just a few seconds of deep breathing can help you create a great sense of peace.

Listen to your breathing...in, out...in, out! When tense we tend to take shallow breaths.

Sit still for a moment and inhale slowly, through your nose then exhale long through your mouth. Slowly push aside all thoughts; exhale slowly, do several times, free your conscious, relax your mind and give it a chance to reason through worrisome problems. Whatever your choice about relaxation methods, it depends on you. "It's not what method, but try and get there."

Once you find what works for you, practice it daily. You'll even find that you're feeling healthier and happier through out the day— less stressed out. Your body, along with your brain, is designed to last longer, than nine decades. Providing that you take care of it.

Tension and stress move into the jaw line where they create a sagging jaw and wrinkles. Doing some simple face exercises can give one over time a better firmness to the skin.

Do it a few times during the week, it slows down the process of aging, it's worth doing, doesn't cost anything but a few minutes, and it can be done at anytime even at work. Just don't let the boss see you making faces. He might think you've lost your marbles.

Dr. Peter Nathan, a leader of an exercise study, says that exercise and yoga may help better than splints for treatment of Carpal Tunnel Syndrome. In a recent study, a program of aerobic exercise, including walking cycling relieved pain by 33%.

In another study, they found that doing Iyengar yoga for eight weeks improved grip strength and reduced pain more than wearing splints did. So take that extra time to relax. If a twenty minute nap gives you an extra feeling of being refreshed, then be kind to yourself and close those eyes, breathe deeply and drift off.

MENTAL SERENITY

CHAPTER 7

Breaking Bad Habits

"Fall seven times, stand up eight."

Anonymous

Concentrate on pushing aside old thoughts to change. What comes to mind to break the habit, whether it be smoking, one of the worse habits difficult to stop; it breaks down the human system and is listed in the same category as a hard drug. Make a decision to be "willing to change." That's the first step.

Let's look at it from an economical view point. If you smoke one pack a day, at the end of one year you are spending $1,500 dollars. And that's not taking into account that the price will increase. If you have pets it is dangerous for them to be around someone who smokes.

Young people seeing their peers and parents smoke will naturally take to it. There is permanent damage that shows up many years later. Smoking plays havoc on your skin and hair. But worst of all, about four hundred thousand men and women die each year from smoking. Don't you be one of them.

BREAKING BAD HABITS

Russel Sanders was Fire Chief of the Louisville, Kentucky. He realized during his thirty year fire-fighting career, fires caused by cigarettes, pipes, and cigars are the most deadly. Smoking in bed, smokers fall asleep and don't wake up when the fire starts. People dump ashtrays in the trash without making sure that the butts are completely out.

Smokers are restricted in most restaurants and bars. Now public buildings prohibit smoking. In fact within a certain radius it is off limits. Some companies will not hire and may even terminate smokers.

For me personally, I have known people who started smoking as early as thirteen. Throughout their adult years they tried stopping over and over. Some never stopped— they're no longer around.

My husband started smoking at fourteen and didn't stop until he was in his sixties. I watched him struggle to give them up. It wasn't easy. He tried stopping six times before he finally quit. Years ago, when they advertised cigarettes on television, he'd watch as a fellow or gal would be enjoying their relaxing time smoking. He'd hurry and switch channels. Guess the longing is always there.

My dearest girlfriend was hospitalized, being tested for a throat infection. She begged for a cigarette in between coughing her head off. Can you believe? Smoking is the number one killer. It is in the same category as a dangerous drug.

Once you realize that you are not a helpless victim of your own thoughts, that you have released any and all emotional attachments allowing it to be just a memory and nothing more, progress is taking place. You are on your way to a healthier beginning, making you free and in control. That's the key— to be in control.

When was the last time you made a promise to change a habit? Are any of your bad habits rubbing off on any people in your household? On your children? Children respond to their surroundings, who their parents are, the good and the bad. A child seeing his father or mother smoke or drink will do what they witness. Those imprints on the brain are hard to ignore.

If someone handed you a butcher knife and said, "Stab yourself now!" You'd look at that person and think they'd lost their mind. Well think how crazy you are when you smoke, which can kill you!

Our bodies are our temple. It is the only one will ever have. If we don't cherish it we will pay the consequence. If we take care of our body, it will last longer, be healthier looking, stay younger and reward us with much happiness.

Keep that tiny word, "try" in mind. It gives one a sense of being in control. No longer afraid of the outcome, it instills belief you can, and as long as you believe, you have reason for trying. The results seen are positive.

Open your eyes; it is the same stupidity hanging onto something that kills, taking a chance daily, that you will not be one of the unlucky ones that come down with an incurable disease. I repeat, ask yourself, "What am I doing that is shortening my life span, that is any different than letting someone kill me by their hand?"

The effort is minimum, the lowest possible degree staying with it, keep the good thoughts flowing which helps in maintaining what you want. You make the choice. Only you can change your frame of mind, which takes courage and determination. Letting go of your negative habit, is hard, but it isn't impossible. Choice is yours. Mind over matter is your decision.

The Dalai Lama was asked about some negative behaviors, and how ways of thinking are formed, and why it is so difficult for some to stop change. Why are some people resistant to change?

His answer was, because we become through constant familiarity, one needs to establish new behavior patterns. Where you keep your cigarettes handy to get to, change it. If you must have one after a meal, stop and change your pattern. Be aware and set yourself to tapering down with one less daily until your craving is nil.

The Dalai Lama referred to the same constant behavior—conciseness, change takes diligent thought. Mental development takes time. By making steady effort, one can overcome any form of negative conditioning and positive changes in their lives. But genuine change does takes effort and commitment to bring about new behavior patterns in the brain.

Truly flexible personal change comes from within. If you are rigid, sitting on the fence, and vacillate with the thought, "I'd like to give these darn things up! Can't— won't give them up!" Being indecisive, unsure you are not willing to give up smoking yet. Every puff you are inhaling those poisons from the tiny, harmless looking cigarette can be a matter of survival. A mind that is flexible, and mind that is adaptable is not ambivalent. It can assimilate change and you have a better chance to survive.

STAY YOUNG TO 100

You are playing Russian Roulette with your health, pushing age if lucky, before your time. It is through effort as well as alternative and wise thinking that change of behavior will succeed. What you can be and can do is mostly determined by the degree of self-limitation which you put on yourself. Keep using the word, "should...I should be strong, for my life is at stake!

BREAKING BAD HABITS

CHAPTER 8

Controlling Emotions

"**Your mind is a tool you can choose to use as you wish.**"

Anonymous

Controlling emotions is hard, it is human nature to worry, almost as natural as it is to breathe. Worry destroys self-confidence, and lessens your enthusiasm, causing you to be undecided about things. Worries, fear, stress, all go hand in hand. The reason to worry is that you haven't learned to control your emotions. You can help this if you get better acquainted with yourself, so that you better understand the reason for your worrying.

We think in terms of mental pictures that are stored in the subconscious mind for many years. Your subconscious contains a record of your every thought and act. It controls every part of the functioning of your body and mind. For one it might be you haven't learned to control your emotions.

The right mental attitude can lift a burden from your mind and body and will let you enjoy life, relieving tension and worry. More studies are being done on the functioning of the complex anatomical structures of this complex system. When some of the mysteries disappear, we will better understand the nervous system.

Without getting too technical, we all agree there are many mysteries still, but we do know using common reasoning, we keep in mind there are only two ways of thinking— negative or positive. Which one will keep us healthy and hold back time if we understand the working of our thought process and set a course of daily thinking and actions?

Research shows us how we function under stress and how some people bounce back, not dwelling on the consequences, pushing those negative thoughts away.

A newly coined 21st century phrase is two words— cool it! It probably started in the sixties. Saying this phrase should get you thinking. If a problem entered your life and you became up-tight and tense, it helps to keep your brain mentally cool as possible. If you think calmly as possible and don't act emotionally, then the mind can sort out and figure out what to do. But if you are going off in all directions, you are in an unreasonable frame of mind. Your brain is "hot" not able to think "cool!"

Don't wait to be faced with a crisis before you realize,\ you have mental resources and power within you. All resources are in your mind. There seems to be a key that psychologists have found, that makes people stay mentally strong, thinking positive while others, under the same conditions fall apart.

And so we wonder. Much has to do with each one's sensitivity, how touched physically and emotionally when very young, plays a part.

Six steps for a daily healthy approach:

"Activities": Staying busy with things besides work....

"Optimism": To expect the best ....

"Toughness": Is the spirit of people who show this toughness under daily pressure, the psychologists see it as recognizing change as part of life.

"Control and Change": That taking control, you can confront your problems to some extent... control over the outcome..."**you** will **try**" and do something **positive**.

"Faith in yourself": Permit no one to take away your belief in yourself. Without faith, you're stripped of status, taking away control both mental and physical that enables you to go further, achieving a high degree of accomplishments.

Faith in one's self is that spark within each of us that gives us the will, calling the best within us. It is the power mentally.

As long as faith in yourself is maintained, the word inferiority cannot exist. There are a few important tips to rework your resourceful mind with positive images, making life less stressful and keeping you from feeling tired, worn and old—appearing young longer.

I have to go back to repeating that important word, **"Attitude,"** for it is a super special word to remember. It is understanding what we are about and what our attitude is that makes our lives less stressful, keeping us healthier, adding years to our lives.

People who generate a kind of inner sunshine because of a keen sense of attitude make life pleasanter for those around them, and they are rewarded. We must keep all our mental powers with the understanding that some things we are able to control, and some we must let go. That patience is the vital sense of possibilities. A willingness to keep trying one thing after another until something clicks.

Remember that important word, "try." I hope you tossed "can't" out the window by now and replaced with just—"try!"

"Your greatest protection is attitude of mind."

Each of us at some time has felt depressed, tense, unsure, afraid, or worried. The art of making us feel whole again, less depressed is keeping our mind from thinking wrong thoughts.

As long as you are alive there are possibilities. Remember, things first happen in the mind of man before they can happen in this external world. Fear is a mental attitude that can pervade all of life. Worry and fear go hand in hand. All of us have fears and worries, but what becomes something that takes over our thoughts and judgment is something to correct.

If you are one of those persons who read in the paper that someone's house across town was broken into and you go around several weeks filled with fear, locking doors each night, trying each knob a few times making sure it is locked; your mind is giving you mixed signals.

Normal fear is the element of being cautious and being sensible. Have you heard a person say: "I worry all the time!" Without having some fears a person would be a fool. But constantly worrying is not being reasonable.

STAY YOUNG TO 100

Some fears are carry-over from childhood, which perhaps were made by a startling experience in a stressful family. Not given the reinforcement at the moment to overcome the childhood fears, you might carry those unresolved incidents into adult-hood, making it a daily thought process.

Are there fears that motivate your actions and thoughts? Take a direct look at your fears. When you know where your fears come from, you can then deal with it. Challenge your fears; stand up to them and soon your fears will lose strength. Your mental attitude helps ninety degrees.

Even animals show fear. Our dog Mitzie was terribly scared of lightning and thunder. She slept in the boys' room. Whenever there was a storm, I could hear her hurrying to my bedroom where she lay trembling, waiting for me to reach down to pat her back, reassuring it was O.K. She spent five minutes than went back to the boys, full of courage with restored confidence. Building confidence overcomes doubts, it all ties in together. Fear must be dealt with or it takes over—it destroys confidence.

When we were going on our honeymoon, driving from Chicago to New Orleans, my husband was tired and asked if I would take over. In the month of February when the weather is on and off snowy the highway in some places were icy. I caught a slick spot, and the car skidded across the road, flipped over into a ditch and started to catch fire. It was lucky we just missed an oncoming car. The two fellows pulled us out just in the nick of time.

To try and find words to describe what the after affects had to my psyche, about driving again is hard to explain. Every day Sam encouraged me, insisted on making sure I was driving. Reliving all my horrific moments, my entire body trembled as I drove. Slowly over a period of weeks, I was no longer afraid to drive—my confidence was restored. If he hadn't insisted on my getting behind the wheel, my fears would have continued taking me over.

When my husband first started in the plumbing business, he naturally needed more customers. I became aware that on many occasions, he would drive around the block several times before he had the courage to enter a building, and leave his business card. There were thoughts behind his fears, that he looked too immature to have the ability to run a successful business. He started out with negative thoughts. Eventually he faced the situation and realized his fears were unwarranted. He gradually pushed doubts aside, gained confidence, and gained a customer.

Fear comes about from your inability to face a definite situation. It is very defeating. It conquers every thought pattern. As was once said, there is much to living life without anxiety, or fear because when you rationalize, half of our fears are baseless, and the other half without credit.

Fear destroys judgment. Judgment is a process of the mind's ability to think in a logical way and make sound decisions. Poor judgment it lowers the decision-making process, which in the long run success depends on the percentage of your ability to make right decisions. So any element that interferes with sound judgment must be eliminated if one wishes to succeed.

Everyone worries, it's widespread. We live in a time that makes us anxious. There are many things to worry about. It can become a habitual response or reaction. In overcoming worry ask yourself; listen to your inner-voice. Start thinking reasonable—positive.

"Am I being sensible?"

Stress comes in many different reasons. When upset with someone or something take a new approach. Try hard not to permit yourself to get upset as you formally let happen. Visualize something serene with the focus— peaceful image. With peaceful thoughts, you will feel emotionally calmer. Turn away your hurt feelings. Turn your attention other than self, start maintaining an attitude. By feeding into your mind a better positive attitude, you will see healthy benefits.

If you were to relate to someone you admire, their characteristic seems to be on good terms with life, you might have to say, they have a certain "emotional elasticity." They have good recuperative powers; they move forward and accept whatever lies ahead. They seem strong, courageous, not dwelling of past mistakes, but are flexible and have emotional elasticity.

It's called the recuperative mind. Such a person with emotional resources can afford to give of their talents, their energy; for even if not successful in their efforts, that personality can find ways to search within themselves, to bounce back and give positive energy.

Self knowledge tells us what we are and what we ought to be, in order to live useful and happier. Ask yourself what you have learned in all the years about self—what are you about? Do you really know?

So I have to ask, are you one of those people who drive themselves hard out to a day of meetings, running everybody's errands, chauffeuring the children to all the things signed up for? Did you say "yes?" You're one person doing everything yourself trying to do two meaningful things at once? Self-care is important.

Make a plan, write some tasks down, and drop a few things. The best ones to drop are the "unreasonable expectations," you place on yourself. There is so much in a day that is tension filled. I compare the life today with all the modern conveniences and my mother's generation; it's like night and day. Though we have great efficient implements, there's still seems little time for self. We keep finding ways to do more in the course of a day, taxing our bodies to the limit leaving little time to relax and enjoy life.

Tomorrow isn't a promise. So make the best out of today. If you mentally picture a continuation of a happy frame for another day and another, into your future — you're ahead. One thing, if your priorities shift, find the best use of your time. Don't drive yourself crazy. You have one body and one life. You can make your life good or not. It is up to you!

My children and theirs never realize that life wasn't always their way; we're not going back so long in time. Once change was about it came rapidly. Now living in the 21st Century with it all, and I say all in the broadest sense, you would think there would be more time "for self." But today we're all caught up in a faster tempo, with needs never seemingly to be met, our schedule pile high of things to do, never ever catching up. It's like the dog trying to catch its tail.

I go to a Beauty Salon, distances isn't a matter to be considered. My friends ask—"why?" The drive takes me into the country, to open rolling fields, so peaceful, so relaxing. Those fragrant smells of newly mowed hay fill my lungs, bringing back my days living out west on the ranch. It is much too simple, too hard to explain. It is my moment feeling rejuvenated.

I know what gives me peace of mind. I am relaxed and happy.

CHAPTER 9

Good Foods-Good looks

"What you don't put in your face can't add pounds some other place."

Anonymous

You'll look good if you watch what you consume. We are an over-eat nation. I have to admit of mindless eaters. Are you one of those that are always concerned, always watching their weight on the plus side? Some of the problems we inherit. Still you need to have mind over matter and put a zipper on your mouth.

I've traveled quite a lot over seas and I find it is interesting what people eat in different parts of the world. Studies prove that in Japan, people eat a bowl of Miso Soup daily. It is made from fermented soybean product and is an antioxidant.

Miso Soup helps protect the fats in the body from becoming rancid. Miso's antioxidant power comes from common soybean. It is recommended drinking a cup of soy milk, or eating three ounces of tofu every day. Many wonderful recipes are made with tofu. Americans eat very little soybean foods. Studies have shown that if you add it to your diet it will help deter aging diseases. You and you alone are responsible maintaining good health, which takes very little effort.

To maintain bone strength as you age you need magnesium, as well as calcium. Osteoporosis is prone in women after a long-term deficiency of magnesium.

Useful tips: **Foods that are essential to one's health:**

Protein: You get protein from chicken, eggs, navy beans, salmon, lean beef. If you are a vegetarian, you should supplement your diets with protein powders and soy foods.

Salmon: both canned or fresh contains the most protective compounds. Eat more fish; the oil found in fish has an anti-inflammatory effect. Eating fish three times a week will help your skin.

Berries: fresh or frozen strawberries, blueberries, raspberries and blackberries should be part of your diet. Recommended is one-quarter cup of berries.

Dark green vegetables: arugula, romaine, spinach and broccoli all antioxidants. **Olive oil,** cook with or use in salad dressing.

Medicinal herbs, are rich in antioxidants that keep you healthy and slow down the aging process. They prevent age-related problems, such as high blood pressure and arthritis. For pain from arthritis try taking

Celery Seed, it can reduce pain and can be bought in capsule form at any health food store. The chemicals in celery seed make blood vessels relax and open.

Garlic, is good for cholesterol and helps lower blood pressure.

Milk Thistle protects and is good for the liver. Plus, a large list of foods. Of course vitamins are for the general well- being and staying healthy.

Fish Oil: Omega-3 Fatty Acids, may reduce the risk of Heart Disease.

Parsley is remarkable. Don't just use to garnish a plate of food, eat it, it contains four minerals: **Calcium, Copper, Iron, and Manganese**.

Wash but don't soak fresh vegetables if you wish to benefit from vitamin B and C. Most cooking destroys the important vitamins. Fruits and vegetables cut up in advance for a salad lose vitamins. Don't thaw your frozen vegetables before cooking. All frozen foods are preferable than canned foods. Glass, aluminum, enamel and stainless steel are the best utensils to cook with to retain nutrients.

The few mentioned foods are an excellent source of calcium and magnesium. The best time to take vitamins is with food. If you take several at one time, take them when you have your heaviest meal of the day. Vitamins are good for you but are not a substitute for food. They work better with food.

Some foods for the brain are:

Eggs, low-fat milk or yogurt, Spinach, and other leafy greens, enriched brown-rice, poultry, and oranges. What we do to enhance our minds with proper diet, plus what and how to think in positive ways making choices. In return our minds can give us the proper thoughts, maintaining proper strength to carry out daily how best to cope with anxiety and tension.

Vitamins, such as **Calcium** and **Magnesium,** work together; we need these for our bones and teeth. Maintaining strong bones will help our skeleton hold the strong rigid structure of bones of your body, strong and healthy, and void of fractures, plus your heart beating regularly.

There is more calcium in the body than any other mineral. The best source is milk and milk products, plus sardines, salmon, peanuts, green vegetables, and others. I can't leave out that vitamins are important.

Vitamin B complex produces energy, sexual and otherwise. Good sources are: whole grains, meat, fish, dairy, fruits, nuts and vegetables.

All the B's are important. B12 is great for energy.

Vitamin C can boost drive and strengthen sex organs. Good sources are: berries (frozen or fresh) potatoes, green peppers and broccoli, wheat germ, liver and eggs. Eat almonds.

Water plumps up skin cells it improves the body's absorption of vitamins and minerals. Try drinking spring water instead of tap water which is usually chlorinated.

Millions of American adults use **herbal supplements**. They come in powders, leaves, and as extracts and herbal teas. Before taking any supplement find out more. Check labels bearing a seal of approval from consumer labs.

Do you know about **Kelp** and other seaweeds, which are one of the best sources of all minerals? Pure kelp harvest from the sea provides a rich vegetable source of all essential minerals a few mentioned: manganese, iron, copper, zinc plus some vitamins and protein, all of which the body needs.

Your heart, liver, kidneys and eyes are made of protein. You need daily a supply of protein, for efficiency health for your body. Antibodies, which protect you against infection, are proteins. Better quality of hair, less brittle finger nails. Definite improvement in arthritis and one feels an increased sense of well being.

Low cal: are string cheese, fresh fruit, yogurt, all great to snack on, eating several mini-meals during the day is easier to digest and maintains your stamina. And don't forget your looks.

Organic foods are the thing, a bit more costly, but on the top of the list for health. Apples, a small yogurt, or dried fruit are just some things to take along to work to snack. There's always an energy bar to hold you over. Load up on protein-a hard boiled egg, cheese, nuts in the late afternoon, when energy is waning, drink water.

Mentioning vitamins and food is all part of keeping us fit, staying healthy, looking good while growing old. These chemicals are called **vitamins**—from your food. Scientists divide vitamins into two different types: water soluble (the B-complex vitamins and vitamin C) and fat-soluble (A, D, E, and K).

Vitamin C your body uses to heal wounds and bone fractures and it helps absorb iron. It's also needed for healthy teeth, gums and blood. **Vitamin D** is found in eggs, butter and fish— fresh and canned; salmon, tuna, sardines. If you don't like fish you can take capsules of **fish oil...B Vitamins are necessary for a healthy skin. Vitamin B complex,** is found in meats, cereals, grains, green leafy vegetables, and dairy products. Those good **Vitamin B's... B12** is great for helping keep energy level high, good for the nervous system. If you smoke you are using more **vitamin C** than if you don't. Fresh vegetables lose their vitamins over a week. Fresh vegetables aren't good after two weeks.

If you work under strong office lights or watching a lot of television, you need a larger amount of vitamin A. The best time to take vitamins is after meals for best absorption.

It is said that one cigarette destroys 25 mg of Vitamin C. Help your dry skin from aging with vitamin, E oil. Put some fats back into your diet with polyunsaturated oil, two tablespoons on your salad is ample.

Many beverages have more caffeine than we realize. The bad thing, manufacturers are not legally required to say how much caffeine a product contains. Tea has been known as an anti-aging drink for four thousand years in Asian cultures.

Science now says it so. Hot or cold, Green or Black, it is steeped in health benefits. Tea is the most popular drink. U.S.A. studies showed that tea can lower bad cholesterol levels by an average of 10%. Making your own tea is better than buying bottled. Herbal teas have well known benefits.

Tea is made from the leaves of camellia sinensis, a warm weather evergreen plant with mixtures of unique antioxidants that are brewed when you add hot water. As you are aware there are different teas. Black tea, green tea prolong life and helps keep energy high. Canadian studies found that benefits for men who drank three cups of tea a day were 30% less likely to develop prostate cancer.

What do all of these foods have to do with looking healthy? Well you and I know that if you are not eating the right foods, you won't feel good, your entire system will reflect a lack of energy, you will not have much pep. Your mind isn't sharp. Your body is always tired. Everything reflects—age! Maybe you're not, but one's appearance says to the contrary.

In our 21st century we have become very conscious about organic foods. I'm pleased to see the chain stores carrying more of them. Vegetables are healthier for you because they aren't sprayed with pesticides.

If you have never visited a Health Food store, it is an awakening just looking and reading some of the labels. You'll find it all very enlightening, buy a few items it will make you feel healthy, and you'll make frequent visits.

The super markets now have begun carrying organic fruits and vegetables plus fish, which some are wild from the ocean and some farmed. Some meats are organic, which are fed and monitored what is given. Nothing is given that has been sprayed with any pesticides. They even have Ostrich. I'm not so sure about eating Ostrich. Eight people ought to be able to eat off of a leg. That's a savings right there!

The cells in your body are constantly converting digested fats, proteins, and carbohydrates, into energy, new tissue and bone cells. They need help from other catalyst chemicals that your body can't produce. It was found that eating spicy foods, especially chili peppers releases mood –boosting endorphin and lowers stress levels. Eat a few avocados a week, it lowers high cholesterol. Realize our bodies will not go on for mile after mile without proper fuel. Like your car, you have to take care of it, or when you turn the key on— it won't work!

I learned that organic vegetables aren't the only way greens can make your healthy. Living near trees does your body so much good. Researchers found living near a park adds years onto you life. Perhaps it has to do with the outdoors and you taking advantage having nice open space to be more active.

Researchers are right. When I lived across from Garfield Park in Chicago, I spent so much time in summer playing tennis and golf, taking long walks. It might have helped having the good fortune living a long and healthy life.

Most people think that wrinkles are inevitable part of growing old, not completely true. Wrinkles occur when low-grade cellular inflammation caused by pollutions, too much sun and poor nutrition.

Be aware that carrying extra pounds puts unnecessary stress on the heart and lungs, making it less likely that these organs will survive if coming down with some serious outbreak, like the avian flu that we heard so much about a short time ago. So if you want to stay healthier and maintain high energy, which gives the appearance of youth, watch what you put into your body.

CHAPTER 10

Love Yourself

"Keep your face to the sunshine and you won't see the shadows."

Helen Keller

Humans keep asking, wanting to understand life better, how to handle it better, and be more alive in their responses to it.

"Love yourself" appears to denote that your wishes come first above all others; that you're only concerned with your own interest. Let us analyze how it is being used here, when I say to be selfish and love yourself. You are the designer of your destiny. No one else can dance your dance— sing your song. We have sixty thousand thoughts during the course of a day. With it are our feelings, some good, and some bad. Your joy lies within you.

Many people feel stuck. The first thing is change thinking. You are one person with two hands. You are not anyone's maid. If you have a husband and children they are many hands. The house will run better if thought of as a large company. Each person has their job to do, and when they all cooperate, the company runs successfully. If not organized properly not only is mom tense and frazzled, but the children pickup her vibes, become irritable, dragging their bodies in the morning, barely making it on time for the school bus.

If you're a working parent, do anything that will make your mornings easier the night before, take a few minutes. Set the timer on your coffee- maker it sure will make the smells waking up delicious.

If there are sandwiches to be taken some can be made the night before. If anything requires defrosting for the next day dinner, take out and let defrost in fridge so you have it ready the next evening for your meal.

Think twice before buying frozen dinners. A Crock Pot is great for making the big meals. It doesn't require much of your time other than putting all the ingredients together, vegetables, meat or poultry the night before and the next day setting it on low it will be ready by the time your dinner is to be served. There are wonderful recipes made in a crock pot, a time-saver to be sure.

I was surprised to see while having Thanksgiving at a friend's house I learned that in the morning, she put the entire breast of turkey with all the seasoning in her Crock Pot set on low and served a delicious meal that evening. No basting, no fuss, no bother, relaxed and enjoying herself as if she was another guest.

Be candid about your young children helping. The night before making your morning run smoothly, let each child lay out their clothes and decide what they will wear. The deciding will come the night before, not the morning with everything going in a hundred different directions.

Why do that to yourself? If you plan ahead it will make your life easier.

Help the young by putting a funny sticker on their right shoe or boot. This helps them learn right from left and ensures shoes go on properly. Another trick so that your child will know the inside from the front: mark their clothing so that they'll see and know what is the proper side of the garment. These small steps will bring large rewards and less stress, taking that load off your shoulders.

You'll walk around humming a happy tune. "Tra la! la! la! Tra! La! La! "Selfissshhhh"— Selfish! Remember it's a good word when you remember to apply it to yourself.

Learn to nurture your spiritual well-being each day. You will feel inner peace, more energized with clarity of mind hearing that "inner voice" speak, making you aware to slow down and recognize what you are feeling and keeping your priorities uppermost in your mind. Take time each day to do a little meditation. Be kind to yourself. Love yourself.

Plan to talk to your children about the next day's events, they will like the idea. It is being a part of decisions and makes them feel important. They'll enjoy it. Naturally I'm not referring to your high school teenager but that doesn't exclude them helping out wherever too.

Making a list helps so that you don't have to stop and think, and feel frustrated if you forgot something. Each one has their job to do, what they do best. Make sure the kids carry out their chores…big and little. It will save seconds, minutes and take the wear off of you and keep you from feeling tired and washed out.

LOVE YOURSELF

A nice trick, have a large black board in the kitchen let everyone jot down what they want to remember the next day so it all doesn't fall upon you. Are library books due? Are dentist appointment due? Are lessons due?

The family calendar keeps everyone from forgetting those dates. Besides, this gives the older kids a good size calendar, to take care of some their own dates. It makes everyone self-reliant. It teaches them about responsibility. It helps take some of the small stuff off your back. Arrange in the order what must be done and designate to do them by age.

Another hint making the week go smoothly and less for you, keep by the washing machine two baskets for soiled clothes, one for whites and another for darks. A simple chore for each child young and old will learn quickly which basket to throw their clothes into. It will become a fun game. One step less for you to do.

Remember that these small, time consuming jobs steal time away from you! You'll soon start to feel like a new person. All it takes setting a routine to your thinking and carry out what you want. Think of your household as a large company with all the help doing their individual job and the bosses efficiently doing theirs. Stress is a major factor keeping you looking old and worn. Be selfish "for self" or any other name you want sounds right—it is right! Working as a team makes every job easier.

You and spouse are the heads of your company and if over tired, over worked, or quick tempered those around— will respond likewise with voices raised, and constant bickering.

You both are examples for the tempo of your household. Your families' behavior responds to what they hear and see.

My next door neighbor had eight children. I had two little ones and never had time for self. With all her kids, she had time to take a nap each afternoon— how? Each child had a job to do and each one watched over the other. If it was dressing, one older would take care of a younger sibling assisting— everyone got the jobs done. Mother was fresh as a daisy. I was exhausted most of the time raising two boys.

Stop feeling foolishly guilty cutting back, when just to squeeze one hour more off that busy schedule list by designating some daily jobs on your family will make things easier for you. When you focus on what you want out of your day, you will have inner piece.

Try and speak to other parents for car pools for after school activities. If this is one of the factors wearing you down it can take some of the burden off of you. The other parents probably would welcome knowing that they could have a source too. Another task made less stressful. You will be relieved and find yourself smiling more.

Did you ever stop and think for all in the family slowing down—pulling back, cutting out some activities? Perhaps a moment to "catch-up" on what you are doing to your body—cut back and let the family have one or two priorities— would you feel guilty?

If you can understand and realize what is draining you, but still continue to do everything for everyone in your household, are your actions wise? Perhaps just jotting down, making a checklist title it the "wise self," will stop hasty actions to do everything for others. That's where redefining your priorities come in.

Stay Young to 100 fills your mind with right attitude, understanding self, living positive, relieving stress. All cheaper, with a life time guarantee, than covering those wrinkles out of a jar bought at Walgreens Store.

Sometimes jotting down what we have to be grateful for, then reading them is a daily reminder why we have much to be positive about and a guide to better thoughts.

Post on your Refrigerator:

1. **Count your blessings.**
2. **Learn to feel positive about yourself.**
3. **Realize that each day is ever new.**
4. **The only thing we ever deal with is a thought.**
5. **Only you are in charge of your attitude.**
6. **Remember what we give out, we get back.**
7. **Smile for no other reason than you are welcoming a new day.**
8. **Slow down. Be kind to yourself.**

CHAPTER 11

Decision and Choice

"Common sense is the knack seeing things as they are and doing as they ought to be."

Anonymous

There are two very important words that should be upper most in your mind — Decision and Choice. Each person is responsible how they behave, what actions they take and what choices they make.

Your decisions, your choices help make your life more controllable, more manageable, and help you stay free of stress— happier, healthier, looking younger longer. It's called taking control of your life! Too often your emotions control your reasoning. It is very good from time to time to view negative habits, impulses and thoughts. If you can be aware of these you can realize that you can observe these old faults and start consciously choose how to act.

For example, as part of your larger self struggling to quit smoking you want to smoke. You long for that cigarette you begin talking to yourself.

DECISION AND CHOICE

"I have made an important commitment, to keep my body and mind healthy."

Focus your attention on what you can do now— stay in the moment. Don't let your emotions control your reasoning. We all tend to worry about wrong things. We worry about a terrorist attack, about the safety of flying.

If you want to find things to worry about, I was shocked to learn that each year more than 10,000 Americans suffer from book-related injuries, according to the US Consumer Product Safety commission. Some people fall while reaching for them on high shelves. Start worrying—right!

"Happiness comes from within."

There are some personality traits that are as clear as the nose on your face; you have met this type every day. These people might be called "pessimists", someone who always expects something bad to happen.

People who are pessimists tell themselves that everything they do will have negative results, so why bother? They walk around never smiling. If you're one of those down in the mind persons, you better change your thought patterns if you want to stay healthy, and live longer with fewer heart attacks.

You are literally destroying your nervous system thinking negative. Pessimism is the default state of your psyche. There is the kind where failure rate is high it feeds upon itself. Such people try and stay away from situations that may reveal their weaknesses settle for low-end jobs and pass up opportunities.

STAY YOUNG TO 100

Have you ever walked into a store where the help was unsmiling, snippy, and seemed to do you a favor waiting on you? And than by chance you had a moment to speak to the owner or the manager and noticed that he or she acted the same way as the employees, or were the employees a reflection full of tension as the management? Their personalities permeated throughout each one of the help. Something is amiss.

This was the last time you would buy anything in that store! This was one boss who didn't have the proper know- how to deal with allocating more responsibility, making his job less taxing, less stressful. There would have been a noticeable positive change, walking around, smiling more, having a friendly attitude, making everyone that came in the place welcome. In turn the employees would have followed in a more agreeable manner.

People who are pessimists tell themselves that everything they do will have negative results so why bother? They walk around never smiling. If you're one of those down in the mind persons you better change your thought patterns if you want to stay healthy live longer with fewer heart attacks. You are literally destroying your nervous system thinking negative. These people are failing before they start. They plan for the worst. If they would plan well they would keep their fears to a minimum.

Example: the pessimist has to go to work in an office building. The office is on the 21st floor and so it requires the pessimist to take the elevator. The person worries that they must ride the elevator, "what if it gets stuck...what if it falls?" The fear is ever present so the idea comes upon the pessimist if they go early when there is little traffic the elevator won't have more than one other person and so it won't collapse. They'll get to the floor safely. The pessimist planned for the worse and in doing so have a sense of control. All this negative energy filled with gloom and helplessness.

There isn't just one kind of pessimist. There is the other pessimist who is successful in spite of fears that something will go wrong—they see the worse happening before their guests arrive for a fancy dinner party they're having. They put anxious energy to work mentally going over every problem might arise. I repeat might —they are ready to solve.

Somehow with their distorted thinking, they manage to make it through the day. But by thinking the worse before hand, they manage in spite of their fears or negative outlook. Their called "Defensive pessimists" and use their worse possible situation to help them save the moment.

"Defense Pessimists" plan to prevent all foreseeable problems, which takes a lot of work. They think wrong, have fears that many things will spoil whatever planned, but they somehow manage to save the moment. One would think looking at past happenings that nine out of ten times whatever negative thoughts it turns out fine.

It's important to be optimistic because until proven wrong, if you're an optimist there is hope that there are better times ahead. Optimistic people are visionary and try harder, remaining hopeful with more opportunities and accept how things get done.

You don't leave your life to chance. To the contrary you keep trying, and see that you have a role in shaping your future so when mature, even though we might be confronted with some hard knocks that could discourage us, you remain optimistic and confident.

The only way to keep from falling into a negative trap and that means time after time having disappointments, the important thing, is to keep your faulty psyche from thinking negative. It is such a waste of mental energy.

Choice gives one power over their life. Decision is determination to be able to resolve what is taking place and know that you only can make the choice to make things better.

"It's choice, not chance that determines your destination."

Jean Nidetch

CHAPTER 12

Relax Your Subconscious Mind

"I will lift up mine eyes unto the hills—the sky is the daily bread of the eye."

Emerson

You have two separate minds working ... your Conscious mind which deals with the world you live in, and then there is your inner or Subconscious mind which deals with that world within yourself; a world that science even today with all its research knows little about. It is part of the brain not actively perceived by your consciousness, from which memories, feelings of thought can influence your behavior without you realizing it.

Your Conscious mind is for reasoning... calculating, wondering, guessing. Your Conscious mind records things as a mental picture and passes it on to your Subconscious mind, which possesses unlimited creative power. Relax your subconscious mind. There is such a thing as conscious reflection on events of the past 12 or 14 hours. As it works through your mind, try and remember who and what caught your attention when out walking. Perhaps it was a person's sweet smile, a beautiful small child walking between the parents, all holding hands. It was pleasing to see. Those two gave to the child a feeling of being safe and protected. All these thoughts have a serene, calming response and clear the mind of tensions of the day. Positive thoughts can help your outlook for the day. This is what to think about, positive things—moments. Remember every time you give a minute to anything, you're giving a tiny bit of your life. By being an optimist, you are most of the time in control and want to be, for you are a "solving person," with getting things done.

Time is a thief, cherishing your loved ones, being busy seeing to their needs— a husband, who needs your companionship, your co-workers who rely on you, maybe your aging parents.

This uptight feeling doesn't have to be. Incidentally, the word "up-tight," is a relatively new saying, but people have been feeling strung out for a long time. Look inside yourself and find, what is the cause for having nervous tension. Practice and continue to practice through power-driven peaceful words and thoughts through your "inner-voice" daily.

It is power that makes your mind obey your thoughts. Your positive mind brings out the best in you and keeps you well. The negative mind will ruin your entire day. Mind over matter! Which will it be?

The first thing climbing out of bed in the morning, hear your inner-voice make thoughts positive. You and only you can direct your thoughts for the day. Be consciously aware that you strive to make your thoughts positive.

Smile at yourself in the mirror—that frown causing deeper lines in your face will soften. Read what you posted on your refrigerator, giving you inspiration to carry out the day.

Being one of these multitasking moms, how you simplify by allocating the work in your house is one big way, sharing the duties and not having it all be your responsibility. You should begin to feel a load lifted.

Take the time for self and smell the roses. In this century with the working mom most are pulled in a hundred different directions, it is rare to find a home-body mom.

So the key is to step aside and find some time to call your own, where the family knows doing what you do to relax is off boundaries to anyone who wants to interrupt your—"selfish time."

You might apply topical applications— eye creams, moisturizing creams, body lotion, all of which gives the skin nourishment for the moment. They aren't the complete answer that keeps you young in appearance, but "know how" to: ingest proper diet, exercise, positive input, coping with daily stress, being wise keeping body and mind healthy.

As mentioned before, we human beings are nurturing. Women seem to come naturally genetically to take-care of others, it has its rewards, but taking care of self shouldn't place a guilt trip. Take a half an hour walk, or briefly try yoga, which will relieve any tension you feel and keep your spirits high.

To nurture is to give to self. Nurture is spiritual nourishing of yourself; it is to give us pleasure which can be a hundred and one very simple things like reading, or working on your favorite thing. Go back to that crossword puzzle which you started but never found time to finish. Burnout can hurt you in physical ways.

Studies have shown in stressed caregivers, that over a nine year period, in one spouse increased the caregiver's risk of death by 25 percent. I recall when taking care of my husband, a stroke victim, I was stressed out. It surprised me that the doctors and nurses would ask, "how are you doing?" They were concerned insisting testing my blood pressure. It was very high. I was totally consumed with my husband and constantly was stressed out. I was put on medication. I learned the hard way that I had to take small breaks in the course of the day for myself, whether it was a short walk, being with a friend to spend time and relax.

If you, the caregiver takes ill, you won't be any good for the person you're taking care of.

CHAPTER 13

Getting In Touch With Your Emotions

"A light heart lives longer. Making optimism a way of life can restore your faith in yourself."

Lucille ball

Getting in touch with your emotions that have been shoved aside, you can adjust your "attitude" and will see positive things fall in place. Agitation is caused by strong feelings. Relax, humor frees you of stress. Did you know it takes seventeen muscles to smile and forty three muscles to frown? Grouchy, quick tempered people are hard to live with. Sometimes the reasons are valid. Can you make things better for yourself and others around you? Sure! It takes mind over matter, you can be less testy if you stop and think how hard you are to be around.

Find the root of it. It appears that more men which they address as **"type A"** have this problem. Women feel agitated too. I mention "should," what should you do to improve your attitude?

Anger is another bring-on the stress factor. Anger is understandable, can't be helped at times, but are you exploding for all unnecessary, small reasons where you have no control over the situation; such as waiting in line to purchase something, getting tied-up in traffic? And there's your computer acting up again. You'd like to toss it out the window. Does this make the situation go away— no! How we cope with a bad situation is worse than the condition causing it.

"Repressing emotions we become holier-than-thou; encouraged we sweeten life."

Dr. Joseph Collins

In these stressful moments do you relate to food as your tool for relieving that tense stress feeling? Many find relief in eating, reaching out for those fried potatoes, cookies, potato chips, candy. Stuffing your face with everything left over in the refrigerator. If you're going to stuff your face eat a baked potato instead of anything greasy.

If your average day is that you're feeling fatigue, having back problems, constant headaches, you don't complain, not acknowledging that you have stress problems, because you carry on; seldom take a moment to relax. Getting in touch with your emotions…Remember:

"You are the master of your mind. Feed yourself positive images. Do not let circumstance be a defeating factor for you to succeed. Throw "can't" out the window. Life is short.

Break the rules…forgive quickly…kiss slowly, never regret anything."

Figure what is time worth and how each day you allocate it, being stingy, miserly. Stop and think what is first in importance, second and third. Hopefully you're not third. Make a "do-list" with the important priorities and a "don't list." The don't list are things that keep your life complicated, do your really have to? Are they worth getting stressed over?

Each of us have a creative power within to realize firstly that everything happens in the mind before it can happen in your outer world. Your mind, trust what you tell it.

Reading what Thomas Edison happened to view about the body, he said, "We only need a body to carry the brain around. The brain is everything. Your mind is a great tool. With mind you have power over all conditions and circumstances."

"The mind is you! The mind reacts to your emotions."

Slow down. Saints and geniuses have found their greatest inspiration in solitude. Try getting up early watching the dawn break. Take a walk alone at dusk. If you are fortunate to live close by, walk the beach. Often a better perspective is gained; one gets a chance to stop and analyze what is weighing heavy on the mind and be able to dismiss it. It helps to sort out things while walking.

Is everyone in your family walking around with long faces? Is your family rushing on the go? Is everyone up tight? Who eats together any more? Mother is frazzled. Father isn't around as much as we would like. Is the structure broken down? Are the children exposed and participating in after school activities, filling each hour including the weekends with their games, sports, lessons, or both? Children are too busy, over burdened. I repeat needing quiet time.

When we allow silence into our lives, we reduce fatigue, tension, and we get recharged. Turn off things— the radio— the television—the computer. There's nothing to fear being alone once in awhile. Don't feel guilty relaxing for a few moments. Don't feel guilty not reading your e-mail. It is going no where— it waits for you.

Stop and sit quietly. In a way it is like meditating. On the other hand finding a happy medium one should throw up a bridge to connect oneself. Is there little wonder that tension is what one feels?

Mom runs a house and is working. Dad runs a business and is part-time mom. There's enough stress just handling one of these jobs, but to handle both makes the stress factor greater.

Besides home, family, and a job, many care for an aging parent with some sort of illness? The stress the emotional factor plays terrible things to the body and mind. That mind of yours plays a major role in how you cope. We all have problems at some times in our lives. Perhaps the loss of a job, it could be a divorce, a Katrina disaster taking all one's possessions. How do you rise above any troublesome situation to find strength? It's hard, one can't deny it.

One evening while having some friends over my husband had a major stroke and lost his ability to talk or walk, and was mostly bed ridden. The four years taking care of him with all the problems involved I had, it was all I could do not to give in to despair.

It took mental adjustments to get through each day. Driving a long hours, making the daily visits to the hospital, and returning home late, my spirit broke down.

Again as in years past, when I lost my young son, I was put to the test in a different situation and a different time. Even though my days and years were stressful, now I had better mental and emotional tools to handle my difficult time. We can control the tendency of our minds our emotions. But first, we have to know what we want and then to take a little time to be smart and have courage to act, getting the best out of the situation.

I discovered the key, how and what to do under stressful moments, and that was finding strength in decisive thinking better to reason. Finding solutions, knowing what was best for him in the long run. Not being afraid to take a different approach, finding better alternatives when transferring him from the hospital to a nursing home would be more beneficial.

In decision making times, with no one to ask but you, courage takes over, hoping that the decision is the right one. Making right choices in every situation isn't easy, we are put to the task which requires little delay and hesitation making proper choices.

Your words become a self fulfilling prophecy. Our happiness, our success, all the functions operating are determined in the brain. If we let our emotions dominate our clear thinking, for it is there where we think, reason, remember. It's the real essence of man. Even calculating decisions aren't made in concrete, they can be changed.

GETTING IN TOUCH WITH YOUR EMOTIONS

With much pondering the final act seemed a good decision that took transferring my husband from the hospital to the Nursing Home. As a year passed, I realized he wasn't getting the care he needed. The Nursing Home was considered tops. I found out it wasn't all they said it was. The care was lacking. Sam was unhappy seeing me leave, holding onto my hand—muttering, "Home!"

Finally I found solutions which paid off. We had a small house on our property which we rented, now vacant. This was the answer to my prayers. I interviewed a few people and found a male care-taker and moved both into this house. The nearness proved a good one for both. With Sam nearby it was a relief to eliminate all the traveling time, cutting my bills in half, plus seeing to his personal care. I was in control and my darling was happier.

I prepared the evening meals and we ate together. I could tell it pleased Sam. It was so nice being with him and not in a crowded dining room, which was so very impersonal.

Decisions aren't easy. One has some doubts whether doing the right thing. That's where courage to step forward, relying on your judgment.

The little house I filled with many of his personal things. Seeing Sam's happy face, more content, I knew I made the right choice. Now I was able to have control over his health care, over-all seeing and being present when the doctor came. I was in on everything which was very important. I personally kept a daily chart as to his progress.

There were weekly visits to the speech therapist where he was put through various brain exercises identifying images of a cat, a dog and try speaking the words. I sat nervously watching Sam who struggled with these simple words. Before his stroke Sam tested for Mensa and missed out by one point. Sam had a gift with words. Now he couldn't speak. That brilliant mind was hurt!

I learned during time of trouble, the worse thing is to be isolated. Friends came often, it helped keep him alert. Even if he couldn't speak his entire expression brought a light in his eyes. He even made an effort to say, "Hello." It was stimulating to have friends around.

When my husband had a stroke, it was my dear friends that made a stressful day easier. Just a concerned phone call letting me know they were there to help out if need be. Friendship means listening to heartaches and cares. Comfort when all else goes wrong.

"The essence of friendship is entireness, a total magnanimity and trust."

Ralph Waldo Emerson

A research psychologist at the University of California reported that during a nine year study, "Social connections are the cheapest medicine." Studies show that friends actually help you live a longer life with stronger immune systems.

Friends are your support system. Friends are there to help and encourage you to take good care of yourself. During illness friends help keep your spirits up. The benefits of friendship are many. My friends gave me comfort after my husband died. They continue to fill my life. An understanding friend is a treasure.

GETTING IN TOUCH WITH YOUR EMOTIONS

In 1979 researchers tracked 5000 residents of Alameda County, California and found that those that had the most social ties were less than half as likely to die during the nine- year study, over those who had very few social ties. Some studies in Japan confirmed even more that lack of social connections to premature death was more than smoking cigarettes.

In order to have friends one must know to be a friend. It doesn't take much. When you keep a friend you add to sharing some of the richness and worth to your life. More social contacts, less loneliness, less stress—a happy fuller life will help you to stay young while growing old. If you have just one friend who is tried and true you are among the rich in mind and heart.

I have to say watch out for those friends who demand, who take, not give in the friendship other than memories of the past, staying at the same place in time. You need to politely cut short that old time friend who calls, has nothing new to say but is filling her or his hour. What is said, you've heard many times before.

There comes a moment when you no longer need this friend that drains you. Whether it be human beings or mechanical things, if not used it gets dull, rusty —old! It is time to toss.

If you have lost a mate, moved to a new area, and feel your social life is lacking, look for new ways to meet interesting people by attending events with similar interesting with your values. There might be a bird watching group from the Sierra Club started at the church. Find your priorities, there's no excuse for being lonely. It just takes a little effort to get off the couch.

How you think things out calmly, not letting your emotions get out of hand, makes for less stress giving you peace of mind that can make decisions.

CHAPTER 14

Your Body Outside and In

"Gaining knowledge is the wing wherewith we fly to heaven."

Shakespeare

We can look and feel six years younger watching and improving what we put into our highly complicated bodies. It can help keep wrinkles to a minimum and keep the skin healthier longer.

There's an important simple formula for looking young longer, it is all connected together with attitude, exercise daily, being involved setting time aside for self…eating the right foods, and rejecting bad habits the ones that you tell yourself daily you're going to quit, but never get around doing.

Years will wrinkle the skin—we all will wrinkle. Worry, fear, despair, doubt these turn the spirit back to cheating us. Wrinkles occur from too much sun, pollution, poor nutrition, smoking which release chemicals that destroy collagen, the collagen which connects tissue that makes skin supple and elastic. But that doesn't mean we shouldn't try and help ourselves to avoid them and keep from happening slowly.

An important thing to keep close to your thoughts is nobody grows old by deserting their ideals, giving up one's enthusiasm; maintain your sense of adventure, stay in the main stream of life, be courageous—gutsy.

As we age our bodies need concentrated care, what we put into it a few seconds a day the results is worth it. Perhaps you're giving in to too much junk food and not thinking wisely, not caring enough. That's it— not caring! A balanced diet is too rarely found on the table. Eat better, live better so that you stay and look young, while growing older.

The latest research that I have is the essential component for repairing cells including collagen cells is mental health.

It doesn't hurt to gain knowledge of what we ingest; what we learn how better to maintain our health, by eating proper foods that will keep us feeling good and looking good, go hand in hand. There is a major factor maintaining mental abilities.

People who have breakfast are thinner than those who don't. You really aren't saving calories. By the mid-afternoon your energy is down. To feel better you're craving those cookies, candy, chips for a quick fix. Fatty fast foods can pile on pounds and drain your energy. Breakfast is key, from the moment you wake your brain needs fuel to function. One-fourth of Americans skip breakfast. You need it for you gain energy and it revs up your metabolism.

I learned recently that rye bread is more healthful than wheat bread. Starches in rye bread break down more slowly than those in wheat bread, and so do not produce high insulin spikes. Researchers believe that repeat of intake of these insulin spikes cause a high intake of carbohydrates. Eat less wheat bread and more rye. Improving your diet can slow down those wrinkles.

Hundreds of bones comprise making up our skeleton which helps support our bodies so that we can stand straight, sit, and walk. There is more to our intricate bodies, very complex with many parts of the nervous system. Bones aren't static; they are composed of living tissue. To build and maintain bone, your body needs a steady supply of Vitamin D- Calcium.

In our mid 20's the loss is fast. With calcium our bones stay strong and ward off Osteoporosis when growing old. Nothing is separate, we are a whole. Take something out or away, and we don't function as well. Our minds help in the process another factor dictating the function of our bodies.

Supportive relationships provide neurological benefits. A study on rats have shown that a rich environment interaction with other rats strengthens and increases production of new nerve cells. There are a few ways to keep your brain functioning.

"We are human because of our mind, alive!"

The mind helps generate us. The mind helps motivates us. The simple realization is the power we and us alone make our days better. Master them and watch the power of choice work for you. The head which holds the brain; there isn't one action that the brain doesn't tell us what to do. It is the greatest problem-solver.

If you have two odd facts in your head suddenly they fit together and you are able to see a new way of solving and explain.

Studies show that senior citizens take in and retain new information as well their younger counterparts, providing that they learn it well. That's the key. That they learn it well, and it stays in their brain. What happens is that older people are not learning them as well in the first place. If learned well it will be retained.

Two most difficult to learn and remember are names and phone numbers. Concentrate completely on the new information taken in, repeat it aloud. Write the information down.

Create a mental picture what you're trying to remember. Meeting new people, link their name with their hometown or state and profession: "Jeff the automobile dealer from Chicago." It's association of things. Don't push the importance of your brain helping every which way understanding and keeping it healthy is important.

I always had a problem remembering names, even lyrics to a song. I was alright with the tune, but after a few bars I'd have to hum out the rest of the melody. My husband could remember every word of every song— not the melody. As I would be singing and forgetting the words, he'd be coaching feeding me each word. We made a great team!

CHAPTER 15

Living Healthier Longer

"Some men always enjoy the best what is, and are first to find the best of what will be."

Charles Reade

Dr. Evan Kligman, from Tucson is a geriatrician. He believes that you have control over your aging. The rate of decline is controlled by how active we remain, mind and body, the kind of food we eat, and the way we control our stress.

One research individuals between ages of 70 and 80 tracking them for ten years, found that those engaged in mental exercising, including reading books, doing crossword puzzles and yes, working a computer, did well. If once you always wanted to learn to play an instrument, make the time now. One thing, researchers are trying to let people know not to watch too much television, because it puts the brain in a passive mode, which is less stimulating than active thinking. Think wisely over your daily chores. The mind is everything that makes us what we are. We need to take better care, using thought and effort into keeping ourselves healthy. It keeps us staying young while growing old. It is hard to imagine that spending too much time in front of the TV is harmful to the brain.

Six steps for living longer, and healthier to 100:

1. **Learn something, put your mind through its paces— attend lectures.**
2. **Add physical activity— take stairs instead of the elevator.**
3. **Drink six ounces of juice every day.**
4. **Vitamins—antioxidants and other health benefits.**
5. **Visit your dentist. Floss daily, have teeth cleaned at least once a year.**
6. **Garden, if you have a yard. It's emotionally relaxing. Grow herbs on your window sill. It's, fun having something fresh at your finger tips.**

It isn't just eating and physically exercising, but giving thought to exercising that brain of yours. It's acting on the thought that counts. It is important keeping the mind from being sluggish, so aim for at least six hours every night.

Four most important studies done on centenarians: Lighten your emotional load, eat and drink in moderation. A good night's sleep will increase your energy, make you alert, help in your concentration. Skimping could lead to weight gain and short-term memory loss.

Some bed time suggestions: Go to bed the same time and wake the same time every day. Avoid caffeine in the evening meal. Switch to Sleepy Time Tea, decaffeinated and 100% Natural Herb.

No late TV. Read something, and soon your eyelids will start to close and you will be sound asleep. If you're too warm or the opposite, too cold adjust to your body's needs. It makes a difference when trying to fall asleep.

Try a cup of warm milk before tucking yourself in bed. It takes about fifteen minutes and you'll be nodding off. Try having a mental picture of something pleasant, perhaps somewhere you visited on your trip, picture yourself there.

Counting sheep usually works. Visualize each sheep jumping over a low fence. One! Two! By the time you reach six, your eyes should become heavy and you'll drift off. Don't blame me if you have to go beyond six. It beats taking sleeping pills, which can become harmful.

Don't linger in bed, but use the ten minute extra for self in the morning. Don't make your mornings the usual— "Manic." Set your alarm where it beeps about 10 minutes sooner and selfishly say to yourself, these 10 are mine. The coffee brewing, set with a timer the night before, waking to the heavenly aroma as you get out of bed will get you in the right frame of mind to take on a new day.

In the quiet kitchen sip on that first cup, relaxing with thoughts of the new day, making it a grateful one and how you plan with the right attitude, greet your family all calm and patient.

There is such a thing as priorities and choices. We should pause and reevaluate what are the more important things and some of the unimportant ones we can let slide, not giving the same priorities to. We rush around grabbing onto every second so that we have more time to do more things, getting more frazzled, getting more stressed— hello! That's not being wise. Remember mind over matter! I'm stressed just thinking how we load onto our self more stuff, breaking down our nervous system.

I can't help reflecting that when I grew up no one had a dishwasher. Large home fans were first introduced. Later we enjoyed air conditioners. Dryers came still later. Microwaves, garbage, sink disposal—heavens we can't leave out the very important computer-age, and cell phones—there's more I know!

What about that small clicker, that closes and opens your car door and turns on the lights automatically, letting you know where your car is parked. Time-savers so helpful we never give one thought too.

I have to ask why than are we so stressed out with so many "time-savers?" We should be having more time with all these appliances doing so much of the work for us to relax more—right? Wrong! We seem to be tearing down our nervous system adding more to our daily schedules.

Perhaps that moment all of 10 minutes to yourself could give some thought to self-evaluation where your priorities are. Do you wonder why you're so drained of energy?

Everyday is a task between work and home. You're getting to look beat, I could say —old before your time! If you are not careful you still will have time to plan your funeral.

Stop! You have to make choices. There is a connection between what you want, and giving to your family, job and community. With all the science and technologies that make our lives so wonderful we have misplaced the driving force behind this strange new world we've made for ourselves, the standard of some basics—losing sight of self while usefulness to others.

Diet, exercise and a positive outlook are part of feeling fit. Feeling fit makes you feel young. If you're doing the right things you won't feel old. That's sound thinking! It's paid off doing things right!

Meeting friends that you haven't seen in years they rave about how great you look and even go so far as to whisper in your ear, "what's your secret? Tell me did you have cosmetic surgery?" You smile from ear to ear.

Being lazy and never finding time to exercise your entire body as you age, you will pay the price in stiff joints that are prone to fractures—brittle and unstable. Home fitness gym doesn't cost much; a set of dumbbells, a jump rope, an exercise ball. Learning how to use them together, they provide all the basics that are needed.

I suggest first some nice slow and easy exercises. Work out slowly, it is safe, reduces injury, and is less stress on ligaments

"T'ai Chi" is an ancient martial art. It provides loads of health benefits, reducing the effects of stress. It improves balance, flexibility and lowers blood pressure. It is slow and easy. It was found that T'ai Chi qualifies as aerobic exercise. A 150 pound person can burn 270 calories in one hour. It was once known as the granny martial art for senior citizens but recent studies show that more and more young people have taken to it.

"Strength exercise" builds a stronger body and reduces injury-causing stress on tendons and joints. It increases, bone density. There are benefits in lifting weights.

"Conventional strength" training requires several hours a week, is more strenuous, can cause injury to muscles and joints because of the nature of the exercise.

"Next Easy" first start out with two pound weights holding one in each hand, bend over slowly, lower your body from the waist down —stretch with the weights. This is great for the spine. Stretch a few times you will feel the pull on your lower back and on the back of the calves of your legs.

"Next sit on a chair" slowly move your arms, alternating up and down, do it for six times then push out with both arms in front, alternating forward and back toward to your chest. Do it six times.

"Walk" If you can't walk outdoors due to poor weather, walk around your rooms, working those arms back and forth. Keep moving with those two pound weights. If you have an upper floor, begin to climb those stairs with the weights moving your arms.

"Side-lying leg lifts" is another slow easy exercise: Lying on your left side, prop your head on your left hand and slowly raise your right leg toward the ceiling, pause at the top then slowly lower the leg back down. Do this four times, repeating with the other leg. After awhile you might try doing this exercise with ankle weights. Try and find thirty minutes a day, if that seems impossible, how about less but a few times a week—better than nothing.

Later increase the two pound weighs to five pound weights. You will be helping restore your muscle and bone density, giving strength to the skeleton of your body.

Doing simple exercises at home is easy on the purse, requires no trainer, just you making time, keeping your body healthy. Ten minutes jumping rope, jumping high enough to clear the rope is another simple exercise. Another way, getting together with friends and enjoyable activities is a way to cool down.

If not careful stress brings on several illnesses. If your job is very demanding and you find it hard to balance home, husband, children, trying to cope with an over the top schedule and find money problems an added worry. Try keeping your mind calm, exercise is most beneficial. Actually, you sweat off stress. Don't let your mind work on overload, it helps you think clearly and make decisions.

As we grow older with each new day we need to keep our wits about ourselves, sometimes even brag about what we have accomplished. Little or large it helps keep our spirit at a healthy high. One shouldn't be modest about the compliments received. That award you won, your spirit gives you that extra bounce that makes one stop and wonder, how old are you? Your upbeat attitude makes one guess.

CHAPTER 16

Know Your Priorities

"Life must be lived forward, but can only be understood backwards."

Anonymous

This saying takes a bit of thought. Looking back in time should be a lesson how to live better forward. Every cause brings its effect. Every thought, every action a consequence. We are the sum total of it all.

Defining priorities, making decisions will make things easier, less stressful when you have a plan.

Thinking about your problems at home, away from the job might help. Your inner-voice keeps speaking to you. "Should I change jobs? Can I find a position at the salary level I have?"

There's much of the unknown to take into consideration. Keep in mind that there will be time spent trying to find another job. Searching for the new position, also time spent on interviews. If lucky and the job market is open, what you're qualified for you might get it. There's learning a new routine with a new job, all of which could be stressful and sets you right back to where you were before this new job. So I ask, can you take all the unknown factors?

Wait a second! It helps sometimes if you really can define just what you want. Perhaps it isn't necessary at all to want a change of jobs. Think, hear your inner-voice speak, if I do such and such will that help?

A few important suggestions to keep in mind:

Priorities is the key: Perhaps delegating more jobs at home, which are heavy on your shoulders, is all it takes to making your job at work more tolerable and your daily routine better to cope.

Shifting priorities: taking the time to think it out and know what you want, might be what's needed to make it work.

Remember your greatest tool is your mind. You can think yourself out of your problems, when confronted we react emotionally rather than thinking calmly.

Panic will not solve anything, in fact, it makes it impossible to think. The answers are in your mind so stop, think constructively, be calm.

There is no living thing that isn't afraid when they're up against danger. You have a brain, use it. Know that when you panic, your mind can't think and you defeat yourself. Thinking out the problem brings solutions. Your mental consciousness will start finding answers that are hidden when fear and worry takes over. Don't think negative but be brave, bold and think over the problem carefully. You will be amazed at how you find answers.

If you start having priorities it will take some pressure off of you and you will be moving in the right direction. Only one problem at one time can be solved. The fact that you are thinking constructively will help and give you more courage to tackle your decisions. Following through with suggestions, and living life to its fullest with as little stress as possible is what you want— so go for it.

As you scan back over the chapters there is a strong emphasis on positive outlook, on attitude, being wise, all of which keeps you less stressed and gives you energy to face the day with an all over good feeling, which helps in your general appearance looking young—denoting an effervescence. Positive thinking brings your thought process a series of clearer actions than if you dwell on the negative. "I can't decide!" "Can't" won't solve the problem. "Can!" immediately opens your conscious mind to reason, and to start moving in a positive direction. You will be less afraid, and more in control of finding solutions.

Many times writing out the steps, both pro and con help to make a decision and helps your actions.

I can recall when my second son was born, just two years apart in age from his brother. Having another baby so soon, I was experiencing having problems which made raising two small boys so close in age somewhat stressful.

As the boys grew older, the youngest was difficult to raise, very mischievous, getting into all sorts of trouble. I found myself constantly scolding him. One day after he again did something that upset me and I again lost my temper, I asked in a raised voice, "Why do you do such bad things and make mommy angry?" The child just looked at me his lower lip quivering, eyes filled with tears. I loved my boy—something wasn't right between us.

KNOW YOUR PRIORITIES

That evening with the incident fresh on my mind I sat down and began jotted down at random thoughts about his personality traits and other things. As I slowly pondered, analyzing my notes, it occurred to me how I was making comparisons between the two brothers. The older boy was always easy to raise while the younger was always difficult. My notes revealed a pattern which really caught me unaware. Not so much the boys, but my behavior dealing with the situation. It was surprising how a little boy brought more negative response, causing me to be more irritable, which unconsciously, by acting out one way or another, he got my attention and drew me further away from giving him what he so needed.

After I recognized and better understood the situation. I made time and reinforced his needs, showing that he was special. I reached out several times during the day. He became a different child— I became a different parent. I felt calmness, my demeanor relaxed and my son responded positively.

There is a solution to every problem. It is just a matter of slowly analyzing each of the steps and believing you can. Knowledge of the problem is a key to successful solutions. The mind will not function when tense, only when it is calm.

Yes, it is puzzling having children, and each so different. Some say we inherit characteristics from dad's or mom's personality going back to our grandparents. The genes we are born with determine the color of our eyes, hair, physical traits—short, tall and more. I learned and took stock. Knowing we all are individuals and as parents we must honor that thought, and raise our children with understanding, not making comparisons, but love who they are. The only time in our lives when we like to get old is when we're kids. When asked, "four and a half." When in your teens you jump to the next number sometimes a few years more. What's a little white lie?

The next birthday we're blowing out thirty candles on the birthday cake. How did that happen? We smile and laugh with our family and friends trying to cover up "where did those years go?" You look at the bright glow of the candles and think you need a blow torch to extinguish the flame. Your one penetrating thought —"I'm old!" Remember you don't grow old by the number of years. You grow old by deserting your ideals.

Thirty? Forty? Whatever! Wait a minute let's stop and think! You're in your prime. You can still have youthful skin, but with the years spinning faster you need to keep up and take better care of your body and mind with good positive thoughts and good foods to fuel the system. Not on occasion, but diligently aware eating junk food to fill space isn't smart. Junk foods are great on occasion but think before reaching into those potato chips. Watch it! Be aware of everything that you put into your stomach so that you keep fit and well.

We watch and care for our car making sure it has oil and the usual check-up. We should do the same for our skin. If still staying outdoors without sunscreen and have a light complexion you're skin is delicate sure to age faster.

Perhaps in your teens you laid out in the sun at the beach without any cover. Now you see dark areas. I remember how I burned, blistered and peeled and giggled with my friends as we helped each other peel off the dead skin from our nose and back, never realizing that now years late, to my dismay, I am paying the price for those small skin discolorations. I was concerned and went to a doctor about those dark spots on my legs. His answer shocked me, eyes twinkling. "Those are barnacles on an old ship." Of course he was having fun with me, but it did cause me to think. Thank goodness I never had skin cancer, but it didn't do any of us any good having a sun-burn tan to that degree.

Premature aging skin needs a diet with omega-3 fatty acids and fish oils. There are cod-liver oil supplements that one can take which is a boost for the skin staying young. Lucky is living in a climate that is humid most of the time if you have dry skin. Perhaps living in Florida most of your days where the sun-rays are destructive that's not something your skin can take without a strong sun-screen SPF15 applied when venturing outdoors.

Smoking doesn't help; in fact it wins out every time aging the skin. The next time you reach for that cigarette think— "I'm adding another wrinkle on my face plus causing respiratory diseases."

You have choices. Remember that word **Choice.**

We are our worse enemy and at times we don't know it or don't take the time to ask, what do we want for ourselves?

CHAPTER 17

Think and Act Anew

"We must think anew—and act anew."

Abraham Lincoln

Glance at some of the previous chapters what was suggested. Some of us are lucky to have good genes, but that isn't the entire picture. Having good skin and staying young while growing old it's the combination of various things.

You **should** keep the right **attitude** and get yourself in a **positive** frame of mind to achieve your goal. Only you can set your course and get you closer what you want of yourself and follow through.

There are harmful thoughts, these are negative, defeating. Changing how you think, taking a new approach helps. There's no guarantees in anything we attempt but putting road blocks in front of our mind doesn't get us where we want to be.

If you're a pessimist most of the things you start out filled with gloom sorry to say, pessimism is a default of one's psyche, it keeps you defeated before you start.

THINK AND ACT ANEW

Can you imagine a baseball player going up to bat, thinking as the ball is being pitched to him, "I won't hit the ball!" He will never swing the bat to connect with that ball with that negative thought. His thoughts wouldn't be reasonable. He would be defeating his purpose. Yet we go through life doing just that and wondering why we're not more successful, mentally defeated.

The tennis player swings the racket and thinks optimistically "I'll get it over the net!" That attitude sends the message to the brain encouraging the right actions reassuring —outcome success.

Being optimistic is power in your mind that generates action, it helps keeping fear down. It gives you a healthy mind to do just about anything. Keeping fear down - how simple it sounds. How difficult for many it is. When crisis is upon us we act or react as we did before, but if the pattern for thinking is to act anew with new thoughts then power and confidence will meet the challenges.

We learn about ourselves how we deal and react to problems. Take it from one who was there. Is it to whine and be bitter? I went through a period when losing my son. "Why me? Why take the life of a sixteen year old—why him?" My attitude wasn't wise. It didn't move me positively forward. Solutions were only found when I could think calmly. It comes from your inner self.

The problem buried deep in my unconscious mind when I started to put my thoughts in order not to be emotional, not drowning myself with substances which were self destructive but instead using logic, helped raise my conscious level and brought the problems where I was able to rationalize. Making me move in the right direction, accepting what happened, reversed my negative thinking.

Again not to feel guilty seeing blue skies, hearing birds chirping with the feeling that you are alive and your loved one is gone. It is hard to separate your daily thoughts, keeping optimistic. I remember just seeing newly formed buds on the trees and flowers caused a tear, thinking with some guilt I was witnessing spring with the new life. Stress is both physical and emotional, it wears one down.

"To think anew and act anew."

Dr. Krimsky said that "emotional tensions, emotional stresses may produce depression and fatigue bringing on degenerative changes in your vital organs."

Healthy thinking helps to keep the body in balance functioning. Thinking negative won't help you perform in an adequate manner. If we keep awareness the resources built into our minds, we can do amazing things. We are constantly being tested. The test of life is to make you, not break you, but be stronger in mind. Nothing can break you when you keep mind over matter. When you stay alert, never down in negative thoughts your look, manner, walk— your spirit is one of youthfulness and confidence.

What is your general attitude? Is it negative or more positive through the week? Repeating, all things are governed by cause and effect. It has been proven that human beings can alter lives by altering their attitudes of mind. Remember if you visualize yourself succeeding rather than failing, that mental vision is closely related to self-image. What we visualize, what we imagine— we become!

"Life, can give back only what you give it."

One important question to help you get the most out of life is, **"D**o you believe in yourself?" That is upper-most dealing with situations. Knowing who you are—why you act and think a negative way?

If you don't know yourself, you will have a hard time selling yourself. You can't think you're a failure and succeed.

I had spent six years as a Commissioner for the Rockford Park District in Illinois an electoral position. When my term ended I decided to run again. There was a lot required to get on the ballot. I got a thousand signatures spending weeks going to Shopping Malls, Grocery Stores, and Banks. I was the only woman on the ballot.

I enjoyed my commitment on the board, an advocate for children programs, strong for our parks to uphold environmental issues and safety, keeping drugs out of the parks, away from our youths focusing on making Rockford, my community a little better.

Election Day came and in the evening when all votes were counted my friends and I were surprised that I lost having over a thousand votes. A tight race lacking nine more votes to get me over the top.

I was shocked—disappointed. So were many. All my friends and the staff at the Park office were surprised beyond words. The weeks following, I never felt so unhappy; my self esteem was way down. My pride was at a low point. My mind was filled with negative thoughts that carried with me for days. I couldn't sleep going over and over in my mind what I did, what I could have done better—I agonized.

Each day from the staff more beautiful notes arrived. The Executive Director came to my house to console and reassured me what I contributed those many years. It was very gratifying to feel his sincere wishes and support. It gave me a mental boost. Receiving a letter from one of the Senators on how much I gave to the community helped. The large retirement party that was given for me, hearing so many complimentary speeches, along with the plaques received now on my wall was all very heartening.

"Tomorrow is a new day."

That next day I actually felt revived, getting back control over my negative feelings. My spirit seemed to come to life. All of those positive reinforcements slowly made me realize that I wasn't a failure but was appreciated and would be missed. For a brief moment I had doubts in myself. For a brief moment I had lost my confidence. When a problem happens, the tendency is to react emotionally rather than to think. When I started to think rationally, I started to see a different picture. My happiness rested in myself.

I reflected though I didn't win, I am a fighter. I wasn't going to let bad moments overcome me. Strong of mind with logic thoughts, knowing that I was held in high esteem in the community and that I contributed much, it strengthened my belief in self. The more I stayed calm reflecting on everything positive I relaxed and was better able to focus on my creative projects that I had long set aside. Staying focused motivated I concentrated on the wonderful tomorrows all ahead—challenging.

Like the artist Grandma Moses, who only reflected on the good years and pushed that bad moment with her children taking ill aside. That is one of the secrets moving ahead projecting good thoughts, staying calm. When I stopped feeling sorry for myself and got busy my down mood passed. It was something I had to work with. Like most things which are negative, it takes continuous thought to get you back on track.

Setbacks come to everyone. Rough times, adversity can be turned to your advantage if you keep that proper mental outlook. With patience the bad moments will pass. As in my case it freed me into doing what I put off moving ahead with, promoting my projects started six years ago when I first took office as a Commissioner for the park district, which took much of my time.

When I turned my negative thoughts into positive and doing something constructive, I was happy and didn't walk around with a long face.

How grand to live another day with the knowledge and wisdom accumulated from the whole experience. Did I learn a little more about who I was? "I believe I did!"

CHAPTER 18

Finish Each Day Be Done

"Finish every day and be done with it...you have done what you could."

Emerson

"Faith, power the mind like adrenalin in the body can release amazing powers within you in crisis."

"It is something to be able to paint a particular picture, or to carve statue, and so to make a few objects beautiful; but it is more glorious to carve and paint the very atmosphere and medium through which we look...it affects the quality of the day...that is the highest of arts."

Henry Thoreau

Thoreau was trying to say that there is an **art of living** too. Not always great people can affect the quality of our day. There are many who we have been affected in the course of our lifetime— teachers, friends, co-workers, relatives who not always have said a lot, but they were there in a moment in need to inspire, comfort—total goodness spreading their love of life—they practiced the "art of living."

They unselfishly gave sometimes in words, sometimes their mere presence in time of need was part of the art of living. People who manage to generate an inner ray of sunshine make it pleasanter to be around them and bring sunshine to the lives of others

What does any of this have to do with staying young while growing old? Think for a moment what all these positive inputs have to do with maintaining a healthy body and mind. If you are in harmony with your body and mind that make up part of your life —your thoughts help keep you healthy. Your blood pressure is where it should be your heart good and so you should feel good, live longer and changes to live to 100.

"Happiness is like watermelon, when shared with others it's a picnic."

It is a high rate of return when you give out happiness you get something back in return. "Nurture your mind with great thoughts." It isn't always easy to maintain a happy frame of mind; it really in a sense is a form of courage. It takes constantly reassuring yourself not becoming down, that you can make it by keeping the proper frame of mind we can do much for ourselves.

If we lose our sense of proportion and become emotionally near-sighted, making our world narrow, cutting ourselves off from the experiences of life—the good and the bad, something that is vital to remaining healthy and happy— happens!

Once as an art teacher having both men and woman in my classes with a variety of personalities that one could possibly imagine. I observed much and found the smallest things caught my attention - how each student each in their own way, unaware revealed much of self while applying paint to canvas. It was their inner-self speaking. Like handwriting, which are clues to one's personality, some bold, some timid —all individuals. How grand that we are unique in our own way. How grand we come in such a variety of color and personalities.

"Don't be afraid to go out on a limb. That's where the fruit is."

Arthur F. Lenhan

The vital secret of life is to receive if we are to remain vitally alive in mind and emotion. To become good receivers of experience wise and generous givers what is called for in daily situations.

"Negative views dwell mostly in denial."

Whately

Lifting someone's spirit we can manage and divert our own times when troubled. How one copes with fears, worries, or courage throughout their life.

I wanted some of my experiences, the negative and positive to be shared giving perspective how human we all are with our disappointments, our sorrows, our defeats, our highs, our lows, the parting of loved ones. We must let our minds know to use logic and realize that this too shall pass.

Johnny Carson, when interviewed about his life, his career, and different things that touched people, a comment was made, "it's just not fair!" Johnny's answer was, "if life were fair, Elvis would still be alive and all the impersonators would be dead."

If it made any sense at all how we have to deal and accept things there was some humor in the reply. We have one important thing to our credit—our mind! It can work for us or not. It is for us to know to reason.

Anything that helps to divert the negative thoughts need not be something big. Steal some short moment out of the day and perhaps go outside. Run around the block breathe deeply, you'll start feeling your spirit revived. It has wonderful benefits, reducing levels of stress and raises the level of feeling good— brain chemicals.

According to the National Women's Health Center the year 2007, up to 39 million households care of some relative. What a toll it takes. Human instincts are to care for and be loving. Putting out extra energy caring other than one's own family can add stress. Man is a nurturing soul. The way we show affection can also keep one healthy.

There is the Touch Research Institute at the, University of Miami School of Medicine recorded, premature infants develop faster when touched and held. The healthy ones cry less and sleep better.

What benefits touch plays is still not clear, but they do know it slows down the heart rate and lowers the blood pressure and increases the levels of serotonin, the brain chemical that's connected with well-being. It also decreases stress hormones.

One cannot enrich one's lives by storing up abilities and traits as we might store up bonds in a safe-deposit box, but by reaching outward and building relationships, it makes life more rewarding. It has been said, "We aren't only to care for others, which includes ourselves!"

The brain is the seat of the soul. Finding how to self-nurture while all around is a crisis is hard. But, it is possible to find time for yourself ,and asking those around you to help. Don't be shy, but accept it all. That also includes the kids—sacrificing some extracurricular activity that you should say no to. We're not the pillar of strength that we think we are, but stop and realize, that you are one and they are many. There is no excuse unless you let yourself be a doormat.

Let me delve a moment what might be controlling your moods. Do you feel at times like you've lost your identity in a relationship? Too often finding yourself in a state of unrest, tense for one reason or another?

If you are one of these people who get annoyed easily. Stop and count ten and take yourself in hand. Try and revamp your attitude by doing something nice for someone. It will pay you back three fold with a smile, a kind gesture, warming your heart, wiping away that frown that you have been carrying around much too long.

People who are easily annoyed find themselves in conflict with others. They are quick to fight over the simplest thing, like children fighting over toys. There isn't a great deal of importance. People who are grudge-holders seem to act angry. They're not pleasant being around, a health time bomb. Both their blood pressure and their heart rates rise. The differences between human beings are normal. Unresolved they can go from bad to worse, a threat to others, often the end results negative with no one the winner, each harmed mentally and emotionally.

Have you perhaps built your happiness upon that other person in your life? Following someone else's dreams might be one of the reasons making you feel fearful, less confident of your own ability—"I've lost my identity!" Might be what you're feeling.

Stop and analyze, study closely all your emotions. It is important for maintaining a good healthy outlook. Take a moment, take time and try to hear your inner-thoughts speak.

CHAPTER 19

Be Wise Grow Up

"Even if you are on the right track you'll get run over if you just sit there."

Will Rogers

Emotional maturity gives much thought to how we are able to be wise handling daily problems. "Your mind is there to help and serve you, not to destroy you." We all possess within ourselves considerable potential talent, more ability that is apparent. Can you be more accountable? Look inside yourself and learn to manage staying at peace mentally.

"Emotional"try to keep awareness how when you relate and how connecting with others as it is affecting you by what you feel, your disappointments, and your anger heightened agitations, how sensitive you are.

"Maturity" is the wisdom you use in seeing and use in a situation. Maturity has to do with growing up with thoughts and actions that are reliable with good judgment. That is a prime definition. But that doesn't mean that we are mature in all our dealings every moment of every day. The thing is to recognize if something goes wrong, we're able to fix, it if not, we can't let it bring us down—we must drop it. That's where wisdom and wise choice show maturity—maturity is growing up.

All through the progression of our lives we are imprinted by people and conditions, which add to our emotional psyche, not always aware that what our parents say and do plays an important role in our emotional maturity.

Remember, "Mind over matter." You are what your mind controls. One has to be tough, courageous and find the positive way of thinking, not negative which takes you no-where in making your life meaningful and purposeful, all of which is a big step to reaching 100.

Your mental attitude plays an important role in how sensitive you are to what other people say about you. Do you feel inadequate? Do you get depressed without knowing why? Do you feel up-tight, and get annoyed easily? Start learning who you are and what you want out of this life. Question your actions, your motives, how you act upon a given situation. If changes for the better can be achieved, than reach out and start making it happen. Rushing head long, stop a second ask a few simple questions. Recognize why you act, a certain way.

By understanding self you are better able to understand others. Life becomes less one dimensional. If you understand "self" you have a clearer picture of how you will, see key factors in a situation, seeing new behavior patterns which can change your attitude with a clearer outcome and get closer making, you a happier human being.

We all want to be happy. It covers a large mental territory and requires thinking, rationalizing and have our subconscious direct proper thoughts, letting our conscious mind know how best to act and understand to make right choices and decisions.

Taking a moment to give thought to your feelings, perhaps finding time to un-hurry yourself, finding whatever is troubling. I repeat, a calm mind can get you thinking with logic quicker then a hot one. Think slowly. I believe it was Emerson who quoted, "Keep cool: it will be all one, a hundred years hence."

Your mental attitude is important. Becoming aware of possible causes of uptightness, or perhaps you haven't analyzed it correctly to mean worried, without a job, tense, unhappy. When you put it out in front of you now think about it.

By taking one thing at a time, talk it out calmly and objectively. These steps where you jot down on paper what might be bothering you, keeping you in a state of tension, you will be able to understand more clearly and think more wisely how to act upon.

"Know thyself." It was counted as one of the oracles of the Greeks, inscribed as one of their three great precepts in letters of gold, on the temple at Delphos, and regarded as divine.

The most difficult is knowing yourself. You understand not by reflection but by better knowing yourself, under different conditions, how you react. Cool down take a nice brisk walk. It provides a change of scenery, distracting from what's bothering you. Play with your dog, fondle your cat, talk to your parrot, or tend to the fish that need some food.

Living on our ranch, it helped getting on my horse and slowly riding down our shaded lane with its large, old cottonwood trees. Thinking only of the moment absorbed with the sounds of nature—my eyes following off in the distant sky, a majestic eagle in flight. All these appealing visible sensations freed my mind. I listened to my inner self, it helped to sort out my difficult moment.

Of course, not everyone can break their bad mood by hopping onto a horse, but it helps control what you are feeling, if you think and practice tranquility. Repeating peaceful words and thoughts, they are a quality of healing and altering your mood. Perhaps this would be the time for meditation. Understanding one's emotional maturity, knowing more about self, helps free you from stress and you can relate to mind over matter.

Keeping your brain alert, we shouldn't forget the importance of eating right kinds of food which is mental input and other real age benefits. Tomatoes, fresh or canned it doesn't really matter. It is a wonderful source to strengthen the immune system and reduce the risk of breast and prostate cancers by 30 percent.

Sometimes, if I don't know what to eat, I make myself a quick snack with three small slices of "French bread," drizzle oil on them place under the broiler… heap on the warm bread: chopped small amount of diced onion, fresh tomato, and one small glove of garlic. Sprinkle grated Parmesan Cheese on the top… it is filling, healthy and satisfying.

STAY YOUNG TO 100

There was a study awhile ago, it said that women who had three glasses of wine a week had 40% lower rate of heart attacks and arterial disease than those who never drank. The same for men. Of course moderation is the key. We all fight aging, but it doesn't have to be. So what and how we think, to what we ingest to keeping our skin healthy, for our skin is the covering that protects our bones, organs and nervous system. This outer cover protects and helps keep everything intact. It carries the visible brunt of everything—small and large bug bites, bruises, scratches, cuts to burns from fire and the sun.

The easiest way to prevent skin damage is to wear sun-screen daily. Sunscreen won't stop wrinkles or brown spots caused by the sun. Used regularly, it can reduce cellular damage. How we take care of our skin is extremely important looking younger than our years, but it takes a little daily effort.

Heredity and expression lines in the face, you may alter somewhat with creams. Aging your skin loses ability to hold water, so moisturizer is good.

There are no hidden secrets to stop the skin from aging, but what I have been saying is try and show how to slow the aging process down.

Of course there's expensive Botox injections costing $800 and it lasts around three to four months. Also, non-ablative lasers that stimulate collagen under the skin and may reduce lines and improve skin's appearance 10 to 20 percent each time used cost $700 each visit. None last more than a year, if not less.

Photo-rejuvenation can make skin look younger by getting rid of fine wrinkles, sun blotches, and burst capillaries. Look for a dermatologist who is experience in this.

The sun-rays, particularly UVA, are so ever present that it is wise to protect ourselves. Sunscreen has been introduced in every kind of facial cream, even anti-wrinkle creams. SPF lets you know how long you can expose your protected skin to UVB waves (the sun-burning rays) without getting sun burned.

UVA is a long wave that penetrates deeper and causes the skin problems that sneak up on you—dryness, wrinkles, color spots. All contribute to cancer. Read the labels and look for the words, "broad spectrum" which means protecting against UVA and UVB.

A brimmed hat is one way keeping the sun off the faces. Baseball caps don't keep the sun off the ears where so many cases of Cancer are reported. The Skin Cancer Foundation reports that drivers tend to have rougher, more-pigmented, skin on their left side. The sun- rays, particularly UVA, are present everywhere, so protect yourself even while driving or sitting at your desk near a window.

UVA rays can penetrate through glass. Inquire about having your side car windows tinted,\ if you spend a lot of hours behind the wheel. In some states the windshield cannot be a dark tinted.

To protect yourself, wear a sun-screen with the proper strength. As you age, your skin becomes thinner, and more prone to cancer from exposure of the sun.

There has been a rise by teens as young as fifteen going to tanning salons. "Indoor tanning" can have serious consequences; it has been linked to malignant melanoma, especially when so young.

Melanoma is the deadliest form of skin cancer and is the most common cancer in young women. Parents should be informing their child the dangers. California and New York, have banned children at age 13 from using tanning beds. The thin areas around the eyes lids and lips are to be remembered, to pay attention too. Safer ways to a tan is from bronzing creams and sprays. It looks good, and you don't have to worry with negative results. Today scientists are trying to demystify the secrets of longevity, how to keep cells from aging—they're getting close.

CHAPTER 20

Clear Your Mind

"Some men are born old, and some never grow so."

Tyron Edwards

Mind pioneer Herbert Benson has a lot to say about the mind. He says, "Clear your mind and the rest will follow." He is best known by his best seller 1975 book, "The Relaxation Response." How to get peak performance in various forms from lowering golf handicaps to spiritual enlightenment. He mentions a word called "zone, where ideas and answers to questions come from the subconscious. Everyday thoughts rush you and can drive you up the wall. Unconnected thoughts from out of nowhere: your daughter's boyfriend, her relationships, or your son's tattoos.

Stepping away from problems creates changes in the central nervous system that produce calm and clarity—you'll have better insight how to deal with everyday problems.

It's brain chemistry you witness where the body increases a gas molecule called nitric oxide not to be confused with nitrous oxide. That when NO is released in the brain, it produces "puffs of insight," it also produces dopamine and endorphins, which promote a sense of well-being.

Taking time, backing off can heal both the body and mind to focus what matters most.

Bio-chemist Bruce Ames believes that nutrients can help repair damaged cells and make them "young" again. Studies are being made on molecular structure, keeping cells from aging.

There is an increase in free radicals with age. Free radicals are molecular miscreants that create havoc inside cells by stripping other molecules of vital electrons.

Scientist wonder if there is a direct link between free radicals and aging. Too many free radicals cause cellular pollution that destroys our energy levels. Every time we breathe, we are giving a boost to our cells.

Not being a molecular biologist, I can only report some information that the more senescent cells our bodies accumulate, they play a major role in causing wrinkles. It is still in the research stage.

If it can be proved senescent cells play an important part in aging; not because our cells die but because they stop dividing and start to malfunction.

What would be wonderful is to have "some senescent" cells die so they "don't build up" as we grow older, scientist are working on it.

There's much controversy over stem cells. Stem cells will be the ultimate well- spring of life. Now stem cells seem to have a specialized roll, they could replace neurons damaged in Parkinson's disease or help someone to make a new kidney, a liver and heart.

In the fetus stem cells develop into most of the cell types needed to make up a person's body; after-birth stem cells are still produced throughout a person's lifetime. Stem cell technology is going to revolutionize medical care. It will be a cure for everything.

Testosterone is another question asked, as men age and their bodies produce less testosterone. They begin feeling weak even less interested in sex, and lethargic. Several studies have reported that older men the average age beginning at 52 took testosterone developed big muscles, but didn't get the muscle strength that usually goes with muscle buildup.

Millions of American men are trying to reverse the age process by replacing the testosterone that their bodies no longer supply. No body knows if male hormone replacement therapy works. Long term studies are needed to what happens to men who take testosterone. Do they stay looking young?

A variety of activities including jogging, swimming, bicycling, and tennis are good for staying fit with age. Scientist made studies that the more the brain is given exercise such as advanced education, regularly in mental exercise, learning to speak another language. It all builds and generates brain cells. Playing an instrument, dancing a few times a week, helps.

A diet all high in Vitamins E-rich foods such as seeds, nuts, dark berries, and lots of dark-green leafy vegetables is a 60 percent reduction in Alzheimer's risk. Eat more organic vegetables and less saturated fat. Watch intake of alcohol. Moderate drinking is better for the brain than abstention. The trouble is some don't know, what is moderate?

Limited blood flow to the brain is thought to set the stage for mental decline, in various ways. Exercise aids the brain just as it does the heart, by keeping blood vessels healthy and elastic. Maintaining brain health "meditation" allows the brain to rest deeply so it doesn't become overstressed.

The reasonable approach is, "take care of your body and your brain will take care of you." The brain makes new cells every day. This wasn't thought, years ago. The brain is still a mystery in how it works, in how it does all that it does. More and more is being learned about how flexible the brain is.

I have to throw out some figures: 25% of American adults have hypertension. An additional 15% of Americans have high blood pressure. It all spells lifestyle changes.

Jack LaLanne, remember him? He is known as the "Godfather of Fitness." He is a legend. Still fit in his nineties. What keeps him so healthy is eating lots of fresh fruits and fish every day. He downs 40 vitamins and supplements.

He is outraged by children's eating habits. "Soda pop has nine and a half teaspoons of sugar," LaLanne says, "No wonder there's so many fat kids today—I'd like to explain to every man, woman and child that people die young because they allow themselves to. You wouldn't give your dog cigarettes, coffee and doughnuts in the morning. Yet that's exactly what a lot of people do to themselves."

Soda pop has nine and a half teaspoons of sugar in it. No wonder our children aren't using their brains properly in school. Do you want to be healthy? Two important words that make it work are, "control and choice." You and you alone have this power to make choices to get your mind in the proper frame; to keep aware what actions you are taking and make the best of it and generate a cheerful spirit.

To get you in the right relaxed frame of mind, take some time each day to be aware of the beauty that surrounds you. Let your eyes roam to the outdoors— in spring, the burst of the buds, summer—and fall with the leaves changing color. Look and absorb the beauty of the seasons— enjoy it all.

Simple as it seems, these small mentally soothing intakes will heighten your sense of beauty and make you feel good. Help your mood, keep your spirits high. Think how you feel as you're experiencing what gives you the most pleasure in life. Savor the sensations you feel and generate your happiness. The Potential Glory of life, against the shades of darkness. That's what you strive for, the "potential glory of life."

By applying many of these sound suggestions, causing you to think positive, making you feel better than what you were the days before, you have put effort and courage into the task of making your life better.

It was asked of Robert Frost, the poet, what he thought was the most important thing he learned about life. The answer was very simple but profound—"it goes on."

When we turn on our radios and televisions, and hear and see so much about the crisis in the Middle East, fear grips us. We can become worried, hearing so much negativity. It is very real to all of us and we have to wonder but think—life does go on—it always has.

We can't see into the future, and shouldn't concern ourselves. Living is in the now, that we find our happiness. The happy people are those that live in the present. Tomorrow is but a memory!

You have the power to control all thoughts, leaving behind yesterdays—it came and went. Focus on tomorrow, with all its dreams and hopes. Those who have the will to leave behind, who live life in the present, have the ability to make it what you will.

The capacity to care—to enjoy richly, love deeply, feel strongly. These are some guarantees anyone can have. Surround yourself with what you love, whether it's keepsakes, music, plants, hobbies, or pets.

Surrounding yourself with some of these things, not only makes your spirits heightened, but lessens your stress, relaxing you, and gives life meaning. Count your blessings, keep mentally positive, eat right and exercise. Don't rush your life, take time to enjoy. It brings positive rewards— helping you to stay young to 100.

CHAPTER 21

It's Called Luck

"I'm a great believer in luck. I find the harder I work, the more luck I have."

Thomas Jefferson

It's called luck when you've acted more sensibly than others. "Think" helps get you there. When a problem strikes, the reaction is emotional, rather than staying calm to work it out. Stay "cool."

People always talk in terms of "Luck." I ask and wonder if there is a connection to feeling happy, staying healthy and being lucky?

One psychologist says that when you're happy, you interact better with other people, you're smarter, and you stay healthier. This all adds up to what we commonly call "luck."

Destiny is part of being lucky today and projecting for the future. A study was made at Liverpool at Hope University in England on luck. People who maintain to be lucky remember more good things that happen to them than the bad, that when something presently, they compare the event with the worst that could have happen, they deduce that they came out ahead.

Most people believe in luck. We don't want anything to jinx our luck— we make sure we never walk under a ladder. We go out of our way when a black cat is crossing our path. We feel terrible when a mirror drops and breaks. We moan, "seven years bad luck!" We rub our lucky rabbit foot and hope nothing bad will come of it. We knock on wood, throw salt over our shoulder.

I know I'm guilty doing the same things to keep away bad luck. We pass superstitions down from generation to generation. I got some of mine from my mother. She didn't let me or anyone put a hat on a bed—bad luck!

The truth, you have to make your own luck by working hard, and preparing for opportunity. Concentrate on your strong traits, not your weak ones, and if lucky. being at the right place at the right time.

Martha Stewart never misses a beat, always pitching her strongest assets, her cooking talents. Whenever there is a meeting with other companies, she is quick to serve up a special treat, always winning over the people and keeping in mind her talents for something other than her present position.

She doesn't wait for opportunity to open the door, she's lucky because she has positioned herself. Her name has become unanimous with many other household things promoting her talents into areas other than the kitchen.

There's such a thing as "chance opportunities," lucky people have them— unlucky people don't. Unlucky people miss chance opportunities because study shows they're too busy looking for something else.

Lucky people add variety to their lives, anxious to meet people they reach out to new experiences, keep expectations high, which chances to live a lucky life. It brings about all forms of positive reactions, we feel healthy, look younger than our years. Luck starts with that wonderful word—"attitude!" Studies made show people who seem lucky have an attitude and behavior that attracts opportunity. Those who seem to have luck are effective and happy, and so others are drawn to them, and you like being with this type.

Believing in the right attitude, that good things will happen, is one giant step towards being lucky. Lucky isn't just winning the lottery. I believe you make your luck if you're open to new experiences. "Luck" has to do with establishing and encouraging relationships. If you know different types of people, you will hear about many more opportunities. It brings about "luck!"

Make a list, how or who you can position yourself better to be lucky. To feel lucky you need a positive view about the past and optimistic view of the present. If we dwell on our past with negative memory, that doesn't help us to move on.

It is said that thoughts and behavior can enhance your luck. The mind, with the many tiny electrically stimuli, the many things that one needs to do to stay healthy, stay young growing old, is dumping all dead, listless, unworthy thoughts that crowd your brain.

Nothing can help faster than to let yourself know, "you don't want these thoughts!" Right attitude, right health habits make you what you want. So you alone bring on your luck. Lucky you if you keep your head on straight, handling your life.

If you learn to turn your mind outward, being more responsive, thinking positive—you'd have to agree— you are lucky!

Your days will be more fulfilling, less stressful, more satisfying, happier, while growing old. We need to reach out and find a positive head set so you live to 100.

Taking command of yourself will lift this burden that years build on life's disappointment is bound to reach us all at some time in our life… with loss of love ones, retirement approaching; it takes courage, determination, for when things are going badly it isn't an easy task to keep your mind where you want it to be.

For over 36 years Larry Thompson has managed the careers of over 200 Hollywood stars. He discovered that those successful ones embrace their talents and dreams, and every star has a team of supporters and role models. They set their sights high and are willing to work hard to achieve it.

Very importantly, make a list of the people who can help you achieve your goal. They are called contacts. "You can't get hit by lightning unless if you don't stand in the rain. But you need to be willing to stand in the rain longer than anyone else."

He mentioned two important things for hindering your success saying, "I can't —and having more regrets than dreams." Whatever we want for the future there has to be commitment, passion and persistence. You can do anything with that frame of mind. We have choices, we have alternatives; your subconscious mind is like a filing cabinet, where records are kept of your every thought and act, and it is constantly adding to this record. It is receiving thoughts here and now getting what you read.

The artist, the creative writer, the devoted physician, the wise parent, each has the capacity to take in from his world and contributes abundantly, creatively, the desire to want to help others, enriches oneself and others.

Dr. Maxwell Malz calls it "self-image" if thoughts are negative when it is changed then you will be changed. Luck plays a part in people. Being positive they generate luck. They seem to make the right choices. They feed into their mind they are lucky—"self-image. They play life's game and are lucky.

"Humankind's search to understand the meaning of life is timeless, age-old." Since its earliest beginnings, humans have created circles or rings of stone as special areas to enter into, to think about the mysteries of life.

These circles of stones were considered to be sacred space in which members of a clan or community would meet, to seek support and guidance from the struggles of life, and the process of growth and healing. In time, circles of stones became the building blocks of temples. The circle represented the cycles of life, and healing. The Stones represented the complete and lasting without beginning or end. The call often arose in moments of crisis. They went to find the meaning of adversity, and to transform suffering into clarity and wisdom, helping to transform their emotional and physical difficulties into strength and joy.

CHAPTER 22

It's Human to Fear

"Half our fears are baseless, and the other half discreditable."

Bovee

As we live each day confronted with trying to search and understand our own psychological needs, many times we reach out for spiritual help. Whether one is a believer in religion or not, at some point most human beings long for inner peace and another approach. One may turn to a divine force—a relationship with God. What one decides to follow as a spiritual discipline is all very personal.

Man is filled with fears—it is human nature to worry. Are you one of those who worry about everything? One's fears are deep in their consciousness and strike again, until a new similar happening, one is reminded again of these fears, only to play more stress on mind and body.

How many say fears take over their daily life? Grown people are afraid of the dark, fear of heights, fear of flying, fear of crowds ...fear of —STOP!

No more be said. Keep this list and refer to it.

*Mind over matter...

IT'S HUMAN TO FEAR

*Your attitude is your protection...
*Be courageous...
*Think with logic...
*Emotional control...
*Put everything you can into enjoying Life...
*Stay calm...Recognize that you have choices...

Every part of our body connects, working combined with another part. Our bodies and of course our minds, work at its highest level when we approach it with positive input. It is a constant struggle to push aside the accumulation of years of negative input.

We have to fight it like some great tide pulling us out further from having control. Things can go wrong, leaving one in need of strength and courage, keeping emotional and mental level high so that life has meaning.

Man is the most flexible of living creatures but the great maker of mistakes.

Have you often thought when seeing a homeless man roaming the streets, dirty, unkempt, hair down his back, begging—what happened along the way? Isolated, no family, no friends, no support group, with low esteem, these strong negative images are hard overcoming alone. What can bring him back into society?

We are members of a nurtured species. It is surprising when a parent gives too little tenderness to their child... abuse in one form or another. Tenderness is a nurturing emotion, when one never experiences it they are left lonely, perplexed and incomplete in reasoning, and emotionally well-being, grouping to understand self, lacking handling life better.

146

One can count their blessings knowing they came from a caring home environment. Asked they reply, "We didn't have a lot of money, but were given lots of love and support." To a child that is food for their soul....helps build character...gives stability. We are able to be better adjusted, to be better lovers, to be better parents. It is our building blocks of life.

What we put into our bodies correlates how we manage to fight off age longer. What we eat has a direct effect on our brain. Some foods improve our ability to concentrate. Other foods stimulate memory also help achieve the ability to solve problems.

Try living one day without an unhealthy negative thought. It might be hard at first, but try. You will actually feel happier and even healthier. By turning your thoughts outward, not into yourself, you will have learned to have less fear, and better understand more what and how you accept life.

"We grow old because we stop playing." Don't ever forget how to laugh, it is doing that we live life to its fullest.

One of the heart surgeons that at New York – Presbyterian Hospital Columbia University, Medical Center, mentioned one day how tense he became. Heart surgery is one of the most stressful of surgery. "Doctors are human too" he remarked and I have to find both for my patients and myself, some humor in the course of a day to keep my spirits high and generate it to my patients saying something funny.

Humor helps patients cope with what they are facing and helps them recover faster. When people accept a little humor in these trying moments, it allows the heart to regulate itself and relax, which helps their blood pressure.

Recently on television on CNN, they did a charming story on women over fifty who formed a basketball team and actually was competing in several College tournaments.

It surprised many firstly, how fit and how dedicated they were. This is not a game that usually fifty and older women take to. These women, known as "Granny All Star League" are mothers and grandmothers who decided they wanted to do something and pursue their dream.

There are a group of ladies called the Red Hat Society, they all wear red hats when they get together, to have fun and embody some of the best things about getting older—not concerned what other people think, they're out to have a fun time.

Not to long ago, I had lunch and noticed about twenty ladies wearing large red hats, seated at the far end of the room. What caused me to be attracted to them wasn't the red hats, but their loud laughter. I could barely hear myself talk with my friends. At first I was annoyed, but soon realized they were out to have a good time and they didn't care who knew it. I changed my frown and found myself smiling at them.

At Red Hat gatherings, the expression "act your age," is never used. They believe that playfulness is good for you and that tapping into childhood pleasures is the great joys of age. These apply to both women and men.

The Red Hat gals don't want to put things off. **"Someday, after the children are grown...someday, I'll** *visit France. Someday, when I have more time, I'll study the tango."*

If not careful in what we think, life passes us by— it waits for no one. You can't keep putting off, someday might never come. Be aware how often the statement comes up. Life is more exciting when it's challenging.

Have you seen more adults flying kites these days? That's one way to key into your childhood days. Life can be richer growing old while staying young. Now you have developed resilience and wisdom, all of which you can draw on these qualities in search of new experiences. Don't be scared to challenge yourself. When younger there probably were things you wanted to be, you put off for another time.

Life is never static, it moves faster as we accumulate years. Thoughts of I "should have," pop up in your conscious mind. It doesn't wait for us. If we aren't keeping up each day, we are left behind.

The old saying "Strike while the iron is hot." That came about when the Black Smith shoed horses. If the iron was cool it didn't bend the iron, it was of no use.

Reflecting, one wonders if there is ever a right time to strike while the iron is hot, for that moment one has passion and enthusiasm. Moving away from a safe comfort zone in a daily routine takes courage. Fear stops one from carrying further a dream, what they always wanted to do and be. It has one good quality, fear implants in us insight for danger.

There are every day, hundreds of heroes, and not on the battlefield. Not long ago, Mayor Bloomberg of New York gave a large cash award to a man who risked his own life in the subway when he saw a man fall off the platform. Jumping down, lying on top of the man he just managed enough space between the tracks shielding the man with his body and the approaching train.

When asked of people who are heroes, "weren't you afraid?" The answer was fear never entered their mind. They did what they had to do at the moment. There was no vanity involved, no gain.

Studies have been made on heroism. It has to do with some basic characteristics of the human mind having both compassion and being a caring human being that makes a hero. All through that person's life, even as a young person, had a love for animals showed compassion; could be called upon to help out in an emergency for a neighbors, they fought causes, and might have volunteer for service in the war.

Fear is there, but it is quickly shoved aside in their mind by their honorable characteristics. Being a decent human being overshadows any fear that they have.

I have mentioned throughout these pages that we all experience basic fears. Facing them we become stronger. Fear is apprehension, with it, hand and hand, is worry. Because both these two over powering factors filling our daily lives one way or another.

Worry most of the time is a foolish state of mind! Fear can be a major obstacle to achieving our goals. Children entering a dark room have mental fear projections. The one good thing about fear, it lets us know or anticipate danger and to take action. I guess a certain amount of fear and worry can be healthy for keeping emotional well being.

Scientists have discovered that there is a gene linked to some people who are more emotionally prone to negative thinking. Whether fear and worry regardless is psychological in origin, one has to challenge these negative thoughts, replacing them with well-reasoned logic and attitudes.

If you see a pattern in how emotional negative thinking takes over your daily life, the fact that you start becoming aware has positive effect. It's one major step knowing who you are and thusly can live better with others.

Living with another person whose life-cup is always half full can be stressful. The goal to achieve is creating a life-cup full.

CHAPTER 23

Don't Run From Love

"How shall I do to love? Believe. How shall I do to believe? Love."

Leighton

Don't run from love. Growing older doesn't mean setting artificial limits. Expand your social circle. It's not always easy to connect with others later in life, join something— sign up for a bird watching group, or a hiking group, a painting class, a dance class. People contacts are very important.

There are many things that keep one healthy as you age. Recent studies have shown that a satisfying sexual relationship can enhance the immune function, relieve pain, reduce stress and more. Take a shower together. Studies show seniors are finding leading an active intimate life—having companionship, being gregarious has given them an added spark to their lives. Don't run away from love, but towards it because it is our deepest joy.

There is in the human heart an infinite need to be loved, and a fear of not being loved. We look for proof of love from the other person. We look for them for our solitude for reassurance. How we accept love or how capable we are of giving, sometimes we question.

And on this intimate subject—the science of why we love. Does the brain actually change when we fall in love? There's a complex interplay of chemicals. It has been found that an increase of blood flow which showed activity in the ventral segmental area, which is responsible for the intense energy and concentration that people in love experience.

Romantic love is linked to dopamine, and also, most likely to serotonin or epinephrine, brain chemicals that can produce feelings of ecstasy.

That said, all of which keep your energy high, and your outlet vibrant, which keeps you healthy with young thoughts. Keep doing and stay in love, for that is what keeps you alive.

Jealousy we think comes from a great love for another person; more often it is from a great self-love. Jealous love crushes. It might be the person continually doubts that others could love them. By demanding love, the result is negative. You never can get love by being suspicious, or having a lack of trust.

Love is vitality and restores life. Without it, we dry up like an old prune. That thing pops up again when you think about aging and avoiding frigidity, staying young, while adding on the years.

My husband and I had a wonderful, long, loving marriage. There was respect and trust. Sam was my best friend; I felt that I was loved, as no other women could be. Having a brief courtship, all of six weeks, we actually went into the marriage in the broadest sense, as strangers.

Each day we learned more about the other. Coming together with one's emotional baggage takes compromise, finding a middle ground, making it work. I learned to disagree, without being disagreeable.

One of the secrets of our successful marriage was that we never took the other for granted. Living with my soul mate was one big adventure. I can't say throughout our long marriage there weren't some defining moments, where it would have been easier to quit. To the end he was my sweetheart. Every card he sent was signed "your lover." Even though he couldn't speak due to his stroke, reading his message of love in his eyes, trying to take my hand, he didn't need to speak to tell me what he felt.

"Life is a flower of which love is the honey."

Victor Hugo

Never feel guilty that you have taken a tiny portion of your day for you! For him! You will see a gleam in your partner's eye. Wink back at him. Sit in his lap, give him a kiss.

You will see him come alive. It takes two to tango— do what comes naturally. Physical contact is a human need, as important as the food you eat and the air you breathe— you feel bonded. Being lonely seems to get worse as you age.

At the University of Chicago researchers reported ages from 50 to 68, loneliness had effect on health, increasing blood pressure. Growing evidence linked social isolation to problems dealing with stress, poor sleep, heart disease, Alzheimer's and suicide.

There are more studies that show the more socially integrated you are, the longer you live. Human beings have a need for companionship. Being locked away plays havoc on one's mental outlook. One crawls deeper in their shell, making it more difficult to venture out finding pleasures.

God created you as a sexual being. It's part of who you are and you should accept it. Don't discourage it. Sex is what keeps you healthy and vital. It keeps you connected. Studies show subjects who had intercourse once a week stayed healthier. Man can't escape having a sexual nature and should keep it in proper perspective. It is good if children grow up in a family where sex is respected as natural. That it is viewed, not nasty but a human natural emotion.

A Welsh study of 252 men and women in North Carolina showed that frequency of intercourse was a significant predictor of longevity for men.

There were studies made in Sweden where 392 older men and women, married men who stopped having sex before the age of 70 were more likely to die by age 75 than married men who continued to be sexually active.

Attachments aren't just emotions. The desire of couples to stay together is linked to elevated activities of oxytocin, neurohormones, which promote the urge to bond and cuddle. They are drives as powerful as hunger and as necessary and crucial.

Satisfying the human psyche just holding hands, cuddling, kissing is very reassuring it tells something—"I like you!" Romantic love pays off because it leads to the desire to nurture and yes, raise a family.

Touch relaxes one. When children see the parents hugging, kissing it lets them know that their home is secure and that the parents love each other. That love makes for security in a child.

It is asked, is there such a thing as love at first sight? We inherit this ability to prefer certain partners almost instantly. Do men and women experience love differently?

Men show more activity in a brain region associated with visual stimuli. Women have more activity in brain areas associated with memory recall. Men are more visual than women, probably because for millions of years they sized up women for signs of youth and health, such as clear skin, bright eyes a, nice smile.

Women can't tell just from looking at a man if he would protect and provide for her and offspring. As human beings evolved, women depended more remembering if a man made promise and kept them, and was he truthful. Falling in love involves with chemistry of the brain. If you are interested in meeting someone, in the first place the combination of timing has a great deal to do with triggering the brain chemistry for romantic love.

Keeping the love alive takes a certain amount where couples try new things to arouse mentally as well as physically, such as going on vacations can spark and rejuvenate a relationship.

Take a shower together. Set aside more time, a bath with the lights dim and fragrant candles spicing the room, adding a romantic touch is what the doctor ordered, because love keeps one young while growing old.

DON'T RUN FROM LOVE

A Canadian study of 75 men between the ages of 18 and 27 showed that men who were not sexually active had the highest risk of depression. Like the feeling of hunger, the sex instinct is a natural desire. Love is spontaneous. One biological fact stands out—sex triggers the release of many powerful chemicals. If we lack love, we can't pretend to have it, nor force ourselves into it.

One, of its highest expression is reciprocal trust. Love is not some great abstract idea or feeling. To love is to give one's time. It is finding the time to speak of love in service to each other and to show appreciation.

A recent review of dozens of studies shows that sexual expression is good for the heart…the immune system…and controlling pain, stress and depression.

An article caught my attention where in Chon Buri, Thail and Sai Mai, a female tiger, at their zoo is raising five piglets. The facility is known for nurturing relationships between different species as a testament to the notion that all of Earth's creatures can live in harmony.

And this article with delightful pictures showed one piglet and Sai Mai both cuddling asleep.

Love is patient, love is kind; love is not envious or boastful or arrogant or rude. It does not insist on its own way; it is not irritable or resentful, it does not rejoice in wrong doing, but rejoices in the truth.

It bears all things, believes all things, hopes all things, endures all things. Love never ends. Prophecies will come to an end. Tongues will cease. Knowledge will come to an end.

STAY YOUNG TO 100

The Christian Spirit

Studies about marriage show if you're talking with your spouse, the more comfortable you are with your marriage, the less you look at each other. If not too adjusted, you glance often looking for a reaction, particularly after some criticism was spoken.

If you want to do the most romantic thing just say, "I love you." And top it with a big, warm kiss. There are some people that don't know how to express themselves and do it by fixing things, showing in deeds rather than being able to express themselves verbally. To love is to have a mutual language.

When all the people of the world love, then the strong will not overpower the weak. The many will not oppress the few. The wealthy will not mock the poor. The cunning will not deceive the simple.

Taoism and Confucianism

Jane Goodall came to fame when she was in her twenties for her work with Chimpanzees. Her research and understanding of there capabilities and how closely their emotions are connected to the human species is known for her outstanding work.

The Jane Goodall Institute is in Africa, with her rescue mission team saving hundreds of baby Chimps from dying while forests are cleared. She has given years studying first hand chimpanzees. Baby chimpanzees, beside nourishment, their great need is to be caressed.

DON'T RUN FROM LOVE

They die if they don't have it, they physically become sick. The young ones reach out to their playmates, the need so great instead of fighting they welcome the warmth of an embrace. Touching, holding is what the care-givers must do, which gives comfort, feelings of safety, what they would experience, raised by their mother. So like nurturing, human beings, chimpanzees, live healthier lives—touched being loved. The great Commandment is love.

We are nurturing beings and need to feel the warmth of another. It makes bad moments a little lighter to cope with. When there's love and tenderness displayed in the home, everything and everyone is in harmony with each other. When we experience a loss, friends let us know that a hug is what you need.

In Swedish study of 392 men and women married men who stopped having sex before the age of 70 were more likely to die by age 75 than married men who continued to be sexually active (for women, there was no association between sexual intercourse and mortality). Scientists now have a definitive answer to that query. The answer is yes—very good for you!

CHAPTER 24

Life Is Full Of Possibilities

"Doubt whom you will, but never doubt yourself."

Bovee

Firstly, it pays to be nice, it has its rewards. Doing nice small favors for others may be appreciated and even earn you a reputation as being likable, it works two ways, letting others do things for you makes them like you more because it makes them feel good to help others.

Mark Twain said, "Getting people to like you is simply the other side of liking other people."

Concentrating on the little things can give you some appreciation not to take your days for granted. It helps being thankful. Doing a kindness, doesn't need to be large. It can be as simple as bringing a sickly, elderly neighbor some soup. Or it can be as simple as taking your lonely friend out to lunch, and just listening to her problems. For you it could be one small unselfish act taking time, and could have big emotional rewards.

We all like attention. Sometimes it takes just a moment of one's time, it doesn't cost anything on the job saying something nice to a fellow worker about that good idea of theirs. Getting along with others makes your day nicer. The rewards are many. "Gratitude," make it a habit to find things to be grateful for, there is much.

The Zen way of life doesn't concern itself only with the mind, but regards a healthy body as very important. One thing they believe and we adhere, "it is important and take the time to observe what is really going on in the present moment."

When you get up in the morning, greet it with a smile and a thankful heart that you are alive to start a new day, a new beginning. Be wise, be good to yourself. Tell the people you love that you love them.

No one knows the possibilities of the mind of man, they are endless. Women like Helen Keller, deaf, dumb and blind, developed the power against hopeless odds. She rose, in spite of her handicaps to leave her mark forever, in courage, strength and determination, the keys giving one the fortitude endurance in a difficult situation.

Colonel Sanders showed us that life is full of possibilities. Never giving up though the road was sometimes difficult. As his story goes, his mother was known to dish up delicious fried chicken. In his very late years, the idea stayed about doing something with her wonderful chicken recipe.

He sold his first franchise in Salt Lake City. Ten years later, age 75 he, sold, his rights in the company and was employed as a good will ambassador.

Most of us really don't know our own potential and sell ourselves short. His experience illustrates that life is full of possibilities if one works and you think you can, keep trying —you can! Try gets you where you want to be! To stay creative, not fearing to go out on the limb and explore your hidden potential, is the key to making a success out of failure.

"Dynamic Thinking." Norman Vincent Peale had a name for positive thinking. The thinker sends out positive thoughts and in return positive results. Like smiling at someone, they smile back at you.

Mary Baker Eddy author, teacher, religious leader noted for her groundbreaking ideas on spirituality and health, founded and named Christian Science.

Chronically ill during her childhood, and into her adult life, her parents sought help for her ailments but treatment brought temporary help. Mary Baker Eddy, made her discovery finding Christian Science mid-way through her long life at a time when women could not vote.

Following a serious accident, bed ridden for a time, she took to reading the bible and kept reading on Jesus healing scriptures. She found and experienced a profound healing through prayer. Some sort of miracle took place, and her ailments seemed to vanish. She continued her work, teaching, lecturing writing until her death at 87. She devoted her life to healing people and teaching others how to heal, a system still taught and practiced today. Using science and health, passages from the bible, her best-selling book was translated for the first time into German.

Her study and practice of homeopathy led her to some important insights into the mental nature of illness and cure known today as the "mind/body connection." The Boston Globe wrote, "She did a wonderful —an extraordinary work in the world, she was a powerful influence for good."

So I repeat, life is full of possibilities. Man with his wonderful resourceful mind can achieve amazing things. Man keeps questioning his purpose. What is the meaning of life? How can he be fulfilled? For one, find your voice and be a part of making your place to live and work just a little bit better. Don't be shy, help in decision making. It takes being active, making choices, challenging yourself, and stretching yourself outward.

Your mind can liberate you from any set of obstacles if you will it. Don't put off— now is the time for positive mental pictures generating health and happiness.

At your work, find your "voice," you might volunteer to take on some assignment no one wants. Decide how much you want to give of yourself. It isn't one thing that keeps you happy and healthy, it is being a part of something, perhaps giving time to an organization, helping in the food pantry, giving to the needy in your community. It can bring an unselfish act with much rewards but the important thing is know your priorities.

CHAPTER 25

Home and Family

"A happy family is but an earlier heaven."

Bowring

The word, "home," is defined as—family. It signifies a welcoming circle of love, friendship, security, and comfort. Have you noticed how the kitchen is the place when guests come, and like to congregate? The inviting smells, the warm feeling of camaraderie is all part of "home." The next place is cozying, near a fireplace when the winter chilling winds are blowing.

Each person should know more about their family health history. In the course of speaking to adults who were adopted, and wanted to find their biological parents because the ever prevalent desire to know more who they were, what the good and bad genes they inherited and from whom. The history tells you the possibility to lower your risk of illness. It can uncover and let you know if you might be at risk as for heart disease, and diabetes.

We claim that family is our number-one priority, but most put the people we love on the back burner. True success has as much to do with the quality of your home life as with your career. It is said that having a good marriage lowers the risk of mortality.

Success should be determined by our daily practices, understanding one's relationship with family and yourself. Family is important. Women are better at ensuring family and friends keeping in touch, staying connected. Connection heals us through the same ways as exercise and healthy diet.

When a home environment is tranquil all are able to keep mind over matter, and days are more apt to be fulfilling. With less stress on the human psyche, we become successful in our relationships with family and friends.

Many children are successful because they listened and were encouraged by a parent. But speaking with many successful business men, I found there remained a spark of regret, never pursuing what their hidden dream was about and was left with a fragment—"if only?"

We are products of our home environment. Those early formative years when we emulated everything heard and seen…we are like sponges taking in everything…the good with the bad. How many of your current opinions are influenced by what your parents believed?

We have to question what we've been conditioned to believe. Keep an open mind. Now grownup, strangely we never have a clue who we're about—are we a mirror of our parents? We know less about self as we fall into a pattern of actions and beliefs that have taken over our daily conduct. If not careful we pigeonhole ourselves. Listen to your inner-voice to find passion, what stirs your soul and moves you forward. Fear is the only thing holding you back.

Family holiday gatherings and reunions can be a good time to reach out to relatives finding out more about your family. When Aunt Edith died you wanted to know how old she was, what was her illness? Somehow you never got around asking the right questions to those who could answer you. Next time you meet, prepare some questions, some should be about childhood experiences, and some about memories about parents and grandparents. Ask about, age and health.

Ask about you as a young person, what were their impressions? It is interesting and gives you a different insight.

We had a family club that met once a month. As the children grew and married, some moved away, some parents died, the interest waned. I wanted to learn more about my mother's side of the family and sent out invitations— we were having a family reunion.

It was wonderful hearing each one tell their family history. I learned much that I never knew before. On my mother's side of the family all her brothers died of some heart disorder, including my mother. All their children carried the same disease. I was lucky, my brother was not.

Asking the right questions helped recognize some unanswered questions. Genes have much more to do then govern appearance and personality. Traits have been traced to specific genes. Understanding your genetic makeup gives you the tools to protect your health. To be connected, to have roots keeps one healthy, knowing what we carry in our genes, we can ward off illness.

HOME AND FAMILY

I had an aunt who looked so much like my mother they could have passed for twins. One day, while she and my mother were seated at the piano playing a duet, I couldn't help observing the two, thinking how strikingly they resembled one another. At a later time my mother revealed the family secret. I was surprised.

This person I called "Aunt" was my mother's niece, my cousin. My uncle, my mother's brother when a young man, paid a visit to his dead sister's family living in Michigan. She died years earlier giving birth to a girl, this grown girl— his niece, he fell in love with and married. Though many years older than her, they lived a beautiful life— never had children. No one ever spoke about this in our family. It answered many of my questions.

One is blessed having loving, caring parents, who encourage their children's interests and help them discover self and gain confidence. In a child's formative years having overly critical parents destroys beliefs in one's own abilities.

For the teenager it gives them courage and belief in their own talents to go forward. For the baby boomers, they misjudged how smart their parents were. For the senior citizens, it gives hope for new ventures, never doubting to stay young to 100.

There are many bad outcomes where parents push their children from a young age to get into the best schools. Encourage your child's interest, do not prod them or pursue your interests. Help your child find out what he or she desires, and not some sport that you and their school counselor pushed upon them. So many values we teach our children, who look to us for approval. We sometimes don't realize we're shaping a value system. During our childhood how reinforced we are or not helps our self – esteem.

Kids can handle stress easier if they are warned of upcoming crises as in the case of a divorce, or moving to a new community in a different town. Be open by listening to their concerns it stabilize their lives as much as possible.

We can't live our children's lives. We can guide them, but they must find their own way for having the desire and fortitude helps give them perseverance, and what it takes to make a success. We can't put our head on our children's shoulders. They have to march to the beat of their own drum. Have an open mind to your child's interest, it might be acting, which might not be something that pleases you. Point out the pros and cons of such a profession.

On the subject of family, as an adult watching parents reach an impasse should try, and help save the marriage. Certain problems happen when retired the parents spend more time being 24 hours together in a day. That takes adjustment, many times difficult, and it might be a contributing force making for discontent between the two.

There is a turn-about where the baby boomers are the parental guidance, helping to chart a new life-style, making the golden years more compatible, and happier.

Showing love and caring is building confidence once again needed by encouraging, each parent to step forward trying skills and hobbies where they probably wouldn't take the initial step to do anything.

Try to help by introducing new activities. Getting parents to do some hobbies separately, things they enjoyed apart once will restore and give new input to the marriage. It will invigorate both.

Just make sure you make suggestions with tact, asking permission before introducing any hobbies not necessarily to do apart, it might be taken in the wrong way. In truth for a brief moment, away taking part in one's hobbies is what is needed to make this old marriage get energized again.

It might be that father once liked sports. If he is still in good health sign him up at the "Y" where there will be other retired men having some of the same interests and he can cultivate a social base.

As for mom there are, many creative classes... pottery, painting classes, or quilting that she probably would enjoy and never had time to join raising a family.

CHAPTER 26

Get A Little Zest

"There is no genius in life like the genius of energy and activity."

D.G. Mitchell

Dr. Kay Redfield Jamison, PhD a psychologist, is internationally renowned for her research on emotions and moods. She says that exuberance is different from happiness. Exuberance is more energetic. This feeling is what you experience as a child when you spent time playing each day for hours.

It seems like a rare feeling that few people have a real passion for life. Those that have are exuberant, they seem to bubble with plans and ideas. They are infectious with high energy. Often they are very successful.

Exuberant people are full of enthusiasm, high spirits cheerful. People like to be them, all these positive actions; we see them as very successful; in a way, fearless.

An attitude being anything but dull are lessons to be learned having the zest of life, people go forth with a purpose. Studies show, that the feeling of exuberance, really are the primary reward you get from your brain for practicing risky activities in a safe environment. To stay creative, not fearing to go out on the limb and explore your hidden potential, is the key to making a success out of failure.

Another character trait is combining effervescences and charm; they go hand in hand. Charming people have a quality of sincerity that attracts others. People, who are charming and witty, confident, and poised, knowing to say the right thing at the right moment. With this positive, vibrant combination they are curious, open to new different experiences and possess the talent being able to attract others to them. These very charming people will continue at whatever age to look healthy, and stay young while growing old.

Most of us drive ourselves hard. To recover from overload, drop a few balls you are trying to juggle. Stop! Just because there's always something more to do, you keep pushing, driving and keep depriving yourself.

When you are the busiest, that's the time to be kind to yourself. Slow down. That's when a nice massage is really a treat, not just once a year, but when you need it now—pamper yourself.

Last year I took a hard look at whether, I was spending my life in a way that was with my priorities. I discovered that it wasn't. I was crowding too much in a day, pushing myself and not thinking enough about having some relaxing time, fun time. Going to bed over tired, tossing all night, trapped in whirling thoughts. My energy was at its lowest.

Stop and figure out what changes to make. Sometimes it's a matter of feeling stuck—feeling powerless, feeling scared. That's the moment when you have to listen to that small inner voice— call a halt to the unnecessary organizations. You can't give to all —value your health and time, regain your zest. As suggested before—exercise, get outdoors take a nice brisk walk. Get rid of that tight feeling. Have fun, go fly a kite with your kids. Tension will disappear.

Each of us has the right to happiness, to some inner peace. This feeling make us healthier. Down time brings us inner peace. Down time brings patience because when not pressed for time, to meet schedules, you are at peace— more relaxed.

In a child's beautiful playtime there is great pleasure pretending. There is spirit and joy. Evidence you immersed yourself in a mind-set that tested your boundaries and encouraged you to be fearless in a safe environment.

As adults our exuberance dries up as responsibilities distract us and weigh us down. Life becomes serious, not having fun, sometimes overly cautious never being adventurous. Never going out on a limb, where the fruit is. We become overly cautious, old in thoughts— old in spirit, we loose that wonderful creative spontaneity that makes life more exciting, more challenging.

As a child play time was built on pretending being in that fun mode it took us to wonderful places. Our energy level was at a high. Often times when seeing an adventure movie my brother and I would play out the parts. Full of vitality, fearless, both pointing our fingers, shouting, "Bang! Bang!" shooting our make-believe guns. He would be the bad guy, and we would have a wonderful time recreating the scenes in our minds hiding behind trees—it was wild and fun.

The little girl in me loved playing house with my dolls. One day, my grandmother was visiting us when she came upon me playing with my dolls. She told my mother that something was wrong with her little girl. Seeing me having such a lively conversation, she had reason that I had lost my mind. There was no make- believe in her world, she'd forgotten how children played.

Can you remember when little how much fun it was playing grownup? I remember getting into my mother's closet, trying on her hats and walking in her shoes, smearing lipstick admiring myself in her mirror—it was such a feeling of enjoyment!

Research has shown that drugs can produce exuberant feelings, but it creates a down-side. Persons who, have a sustainable exuberance that can be tapped into with no side effects, that kind of exuberance is very contagious. Having good health keeps one's energy high.

Get that music out, listen to some jazz. Swing those arms around. That feeling coming alive, full of energy, will start lifting your spirits. People, who are full of life, give off some wonderful contagious vibes that you love being near—exuberance!

Studies show that music raises levels of the brain chemical dopamine in a way that mimics a drug-induced euphoria. Music acts quickly on the brain.

If that male companion you know seem to be extra moody, lethargic extra grumpy, or even angry. He might be suffering from **IMS.**

It's known as Irritable Male Syndrome. Dr. Gerald Lincoln, a Scottish researcher, found that when the testosterone levels in the animals he was studying dropped they became more irritable, some also lethargic.

It takes some men a long time being in denial before they can begin to recognize just what is wrong. If your man has lost his zest when he should have energy and be cheerful. When he casts blame outward…they are being impatient, hostile, stressed. They could be suffering from **IMS.** Having a thorough health checkup, with blood tests for testosterone, is important.

Men are the worse offenders, not seeing a doctor often enough. More than women men over estimate their fitness. Men with their macho outlook will overlook getting injured and work through their pain, making matters worse sometimes.

Men should get a checkup before starting a sport that is taxing like tennis, or soccer. Another reason to get a checkup is when that man in your life has gained a lot of weight or is a heavy smoker, or has a family history of heart disease.

Playing any strenuous game might bring on a heart attack. If Monday morning your partner can hardly get out of bed due to pain, this is a sign that he must cut back the following weekend. Convince him that you love him and want him around for a very long time—if anything, you might hint, he has to be more of a help around the house with the kids.

Are you one of these men who view the world through "a negative spin on situations and actions?" Too often grouchy, the male does go through midlife crisis and turbulent times, but IMS is something else. Keeping in good health, and daily exercise is very important and can improve, and once again he can be an ardent partner.

To greatly improve the health and quality of life for millions of people, it is called "phytochemical" (phyto) is derived from the Greek word for plant, and it is suppose to be the next hope for a magic pill, one that goes beyond vitamins.

The report mentioned a woman in her early sixties who ran down eight flights of stairs after taking a phytochemical product for only a few days. Normally she would have moved slowly down the stairs.

Scientists only discovered phytochemicals a few years ago, even though they have existed in whole vegetables, fruit and pine bark from the beginning.

Every slice of a tomato contains thousands of phytochemicals. This same quality have important qualities on human beings. More and more studies are being made on numerous health benefits

In 1535, Jacques Cartier, the French explorer, got his ship ice bound in the St. Lawrence waterway in Canada. It was a desperate situation for Cartier and crew. All they had to eat was some salted meat. The crew developed scurvy because of the lack of fresh vegetables and fruit. Many of his men were dying when Cartier was given a tea by a Canadian Indian. The tea had been made from the bark of the "maritime pine tree."

Amazing Cartier and his crew fully recovered in just a few weeks. Cartier wrote of this experience in his book, "Voyage in Canada" and 400 years later, Dr. Jack Masquelier, a member of the faculty at the University of

Bordeaux, read the book and isolated the substance in the maritime pine trees, which had saved the lives of Cartier and his crew.

Masquelier discovered that this substance had many qualities including, being a very powerful scavenger of free radicals. They are increasingly believed to be responsible for the beginning stages of many dreaded ailments, including cancer and heart disease.

Wonderful things happened when some of his staff members started taking Phytochemicals for three to six months all staff members reported benefit effects: astounding increase in physical energy, mental acuity, including memory, minor arthritis pains in fingers lessen.

Phytochemical products made from maritime pine bark and seedless grapes, which have the same qualities, have been available for a number of years. Now are available in the United States.

Melatonin, a chemical found in some of the foods we eat, is an anti-stress agent and a good sleep promoter. Walnuts have melatonin in them too. Hundred of studies have proven that green tea and its various extracts can prevent and in some experiments, reverse cancer.

Increase fruits and vegetables and your meals, higher in fiber and lower in fats and calories. Fill at least two-thirds of your plate green and no more than one-third with animal protein.

Watermelon is packed with nutrients like lycopene, which lowers the risk of prostate cancer in men and cervical cancer in women. The vitamin promotes eye health and vitamin C boots immunity and fights infection. Eating small amounts of low or zero-fat carbs, you should feel good and not gain weight. But again, like everything, eating a lot will put on the weight.

When dark, gloomy, old nasty weather is upon us and your sniffles are telling you're coming down with a cold, make yourself a turkey sandwich. Turkey is a good source of glutamine, an amino acid used by cells to protect against infection— boosts immunity. So eat turkey often during the cold season to keep protective cells working at their peak.

All humans are subject to the natural ebb and flow of human emotions. Due to the average lack of emotional control, the belief that something bad is going to happen, by keeping your mind thinking positive, things will work out successful. It's when we feed ourselves negative thoughts that we are unsuccessful. Every day there are thousands of unrecorded instances where humans exercise faith in meetings, and overcome difficult situations.

With their own efforts, their own mental attitude, their mental pictures come true. One of the best ways to end discouragement for one reason or another is to rise to the challenge your difficulties offer.

Life balance is important. Stability is another way to show reasoning and logic. How we balance out our days as to what is important, what must be done, and the unimportant things, that we hold onto that should be discarded; giving us more balance, less stress to our life finding more "selfish time."

Our complicated lives pull us in many directions— it drains us. Finding balance helps keep us with our feet on the ground. Let me say there is a lesson learned in everything. You never learn from sweetness and light.

There's nothing like a good fight, standup and you'll grow bigger and stronger.

Discouragement is long formed before "courage." Get your priorities in order. Many of life's failures are those people who did not realize how close they were to success, when they threw in the towel and gave up. Not giving up, having the mind to find choices, being determined, thinking positive, feeds the mind to find alternatives.

We all like to hear survival stories. It tells us what man is capable of. It reinforces us how to live life and not despair, to believe that this too shall pass.

It was refreshing seeing and hearing Paula Deen, the food expert known as the first lady of Southern cooking, on TV. Her exuberance and infectious giggle makes you want to laugh. I couldn't get enough of her.

In her book she relates years of suffering with agoraphobia, a fear of open spaces and people, having anxiety attacks, and not getting out of her house. At this time she went through a divorce which didn't help in her fragile mental state. Conquering her many daily demons, with determination and much courage, slowly, she took charge of her life, learned to control her emotions overcame much and is well, happy and very successful today with her television show and a second marriage. She is a different person confident, mentally well.

If you ever have a chance seeing her show, you can't imagine this outgoing, effervescent personality, full of confidence ever suffered so much, came so far now in the main stream of life. Paula Deen is an ideal example that if there is a will one can overcome. If one doesn't "try," they will never know.

GET A LITTLE ZEST

Self-confidence helps one to succeed. Try is all part of that word. It is the ability to know what one wants overcoming obstacles in the path getting there. Successful people have an air of their own ability, capable of assuming responsibilities. All of us go through life making mistakes, it is inevitable. Basing our life on other people's expectations trying to fit there goals into ours, one feels less fulfilled with few positive accomplishments. One must never confuse one's mistakes past hurts, with one's value as a human being, negative thinking is self defeating.

CHAPTER 27

Go forth With Purpose

"Live with thought each day."

Anonymous

You have a choice to pull back, saying no to some of the demands. Probably you have your self to blame by answering all through the years, to each one's wishes. Some go beyond your limits, but still they are met. Reflect that you and only you can make the choice, to selfishly start practicing how not to be at everyone's beck and call.

As I have said before, homes and family should be run like a corporation, with each one doing their job, not one person to carry the entire burden. Have you looked into alternatives into spreading daily obligations equally around? Trying to please, giving so much to the demands from family— it is time think in a new direction, letting others carry some of your daily obligation. You will feel like a reborn person, energized having more time caring for self— a better rounded person.

Man is a social being— gregarious. He lives longer, and healthier when not being anti-social. Put away that cell phone. Stop using your laptop. Make time to be with friends. They bring nourishment to your physic.

I once worked with a dynamite woman, of seventy years young. I wanted to know when she planned to slow down..."slow down? I'm thinking of sky diving!" To look at her you would say this is a woman of fifty, no more. Everything about her is positive and she has maintained her inspiring outlook. Life has not passed her by. She loves life, and life loves her. She has pushed aside what she no longer has the power to change. Learning early on, who she was with a positive outlook, she has made her life meaningful, concentrating on her priorities, warding off stress. With such a spirit, she will add years to her life.

We can't stop father time from showing on our face and body. We all desire to look younger than our years, but if we learn how to live each day, understanding about choice and attitude, have a purpose with a healthy program; we can fend off stress, the number one cause for aging— we are half way there—staying young to 100.

We know that sun ages skin. Some people seem to be wrinkle free, while others look like dried-up prunes, at the same age of forty. Some of it has to do with diet.

People over 70 who live in Greece, Australia, and Sweden. Those with good diets have good skin.

In Greece where they ate green leafy vegetables, olive oil, garlic, compared with Aussies who drank tea, ate sardines, apples, melons and multigrain bread, they did very well. Swedes ate low-fat yogurt, skim milk, spinach pie.

The result advice is sound whether you're concerned about your skin or your heart; replace foods high in saturated fats with fish, beans, olive oil, whole grains and low-fat dairy. You have to feel good and your skin will see the results.

If you've been remiss, it's never too late, though the effort gets greater, the time for results slower, but stay with it, not discouraged. How you deal daily, that's what count projecting toward a working schedule, keeping you fit and prolonging your life.

They found when military recruits take vitamin C; they're less likely to get ill. Vitamin C counteracts stress on the immune system. It is suggested that taking it after breakfast could help.

At the University of Alabama, a study found that rats under stress who got plenty of C had one-third the level of stress hormones of C-less rats.

One thing more that has nothing to do with what you eat but how you chew your food well. Many chronic problems of the stomach have to do with gulping down our food.

Supposedly a glass of wine a day can lower your risk of heart disease. There's healing power of wine. Other recent studies suggest postmenopausal women who consume one glass of wine every day have stronger bones than non-drinkers. Of course moderation is the key.

How does wine have such benefits? Alcohol opens up arteries and increases blood flow. The antioxidants in some forms especially red wine can prevent LDL cholesterol from oxidizing, which damages artery walls, setting the stage for heart disease.

GO FORTH WITH PURPOSE

I'm not encouraging you to drink for there are many same benefits by exercising, and watching your diet are top on the list.

Common sense isn't very common. It doesn't take much to keep the body from aging. Fact finding is out there, but the human species what they are, feel they are invincible and only bother to save themselves when confronted with a physical problem. By then it might be too late.

CHAPTER 28

Are You in Control

"Don't let anyone hold your happiness in their hands, hold it in yours, so it will always be within your reach."

Anonymous

Are You In...T-total...C-control?

It is very important no one should have the power to rule you, unless you like being subservient to the other person. Remember that you always have a choice— and are in total control of your life. When did you give up your rights to enjoy life? How dare anyone take that away?

When we're children our parents tell us what to do. They, and our home environment, shape who we are—not necessarily who we become, which takes quality-thinking, quality effort. It takes daily process, thinking your way clear. So as an adult with all your powers, you and you alone have the power to control your life.

Relationships, spending time with others, gives us more insight who we become. We never become perfect because we live in an imperfect world. But the ability that you can accept and learn from your experiences, good and bad, taking you where you are now, to where you want to be, involves interaction with others to enjoy a happy life with a deeper sense what you stand for.

ARE YOU IN CONTROL

It takes time to finally filter through, to understand the many obstacles and decision making that life presents. Going through different stages: with learning to do other people's wishes... relationships—marriage, children or divorce. Keeping a flexible mind helps us reconcile our problems.

Testing us by sudden unexpected, sometimes tragedy, helps us more, to understand being aware of our strengths, weaknesses, tolerance, patience, compassion, fears.

As you keep putting out those around keep expecting. One day you realize you've been cheated. What you want involves nurturing yourself, doing things you have set aside for too long, you will stay healthier with less stress, living a more satisfying life.

You study your face in the mirror..."I need a face make over!" pops up in your mind.

Who of us haven't liked what we see? But, we can help ourselves with what we feed our minds, with positive attitudes. And feed our systems with proper diet. And conduct our lives with as little stress as we can help to live life happy. All of which makes for a better appearance.

The latest statistics, each year more than 70,000 people (93%) women get face-lifts. I recently learned more from a cosmetic surgeon. It's questionable; can a face-lift make you look younger? What is known is that it can establish youthful facial contours by correcting sagging cheeks, a double chin, but it won't remove most wrinkles.

Surgeons without proper experience try to remove wrinkles by pulling the skin too tight, giving the patient an artificial look. The potential risk of cosmetic surgery is there. Going under the knife is always some risk.

If you mustered courage, make sure you find a top cosmetic surgeon...not the cheapest, a super specialist who performs only facial cosmetic surgery, board-certified in plastic or head surgery, with at least ten years in his field.

Get one that uses computer imaging showing you the now and what you will visualize after the corrections. If you are not satisfied, let your feelings be known. Do not be shy, you have only one face. Be open and let the doctor know what you are feeling— after it is too late. It took a certain amount of courage to even contemplate this big step. And I repeat—this big step.

Let me tell you about the operations procedure, decide if this is the way to go. It takes three to five hours. The patient is given a general anesthetic by a board certified anesthesiologist or a certified registered nurse.

Incisions are made within the hairline and hidden in the ear contours and below the chin. Fatty tissue is sculpted or repositioned. Muscles tightened and excess skin trimmed away and the remainder skin rearranged. Most bruising and puffiness is gone within two weeks, pain minimal. But I must mention again, it can be dangerous with the outcome not always successful.

The cost usually is not covered by insurance. Are you sitting down, ready to hear this? Between $10,000 and $20,000 depending on what exactly you are having done. Sometimes it can be lower, when there is a cancellation, getting the surgery on a standby basis. You could save around 10%.

One of the more risky ways to save money to have what is called, a "vacation face-lift" that is going to

Argentina, Mexico or another country. Safety standards are not up to US standards, be very cautious.

And if you have to return because of complications there are more costs involved. So when you first thought of saving money, think twice.

I have known a few friends and relatives that had cosmetic surgery. A cousin who had her eyes done, had to redo to correct faulty surgery. There are risks going under the knife. There's no risk if you just use a topical applications. Applying makeup can restore your image and make you less critical of self and much less intrusive.

Let's call it the 21st Century make-over. What we have in investment is minimal and a darn sight safer.

A few cosmetic hints:

Applying on a layer of foundation or powder only makes wrinkles stand out more. Use a concealer, it hides any darkness or redness and makes the skin void of blemishes and helps you look more youthful.

Applied a light, concealer, to the inner corner of your eye lids brightens up the eye area. With eye pencil define your upper lash line, use the line thin. Light eye shadow attracts light, makes the eyes look bright. A well defined brow is essential. As we age—our hair, brow, lashes are now thinner. Fill in the sparse areas with a brow pencil. Apply two coats of black mascara on the upper lashes. It brings out the eyes.

Add cheek color, it is very essential. Sweep a bronzer with peach undertones on the apple of your cheeks. Start with a cream blush in a shade that matches your skin's natural flush. A creamy texture is ideal for older, drier skin. If not applying with a brush, blend with your fingers.

Take a darker foundation or powder and rub it along your neck and right underneath your jaw. That helps camouflage some of the flab.

With age tiny lines start to appear around the lips. Use a lip –liner begin with a lip pencil, use brighter shades…cranberry and berry lip gloss, lipsticks really complement fading skin tones.

Don't stop there. Your hair color can make you look so much younger. Whatever your hair color used to be, go a few shades lighter, add a few highlights. While thinking about hair, find another cut. Getting a new style does wonders for your appearance. Go to a Salon that knows something about hair. A new hair style is a definite up-lift. Your old friends will be amazed and whisper in your ear— "tell me did you have cosmetic surgery?" Your new general appearance— color in the face color to your hair will give you an added boost. That's what you want. With little effort it can take you from feeling down to putting on a new face with positive feed back. Your wrinkles may still be there, not as pronounced, as you distracted where the eye looks.

CHAPTER 29

Criticism Hard To Take

"It's better to bite your tongue than eat your words."

Bovee

Life is difficult enough without hateful, jealous people trying to hurt you. Ann Landers said in her column, "hate is like acid, it can destroy the pitcher which it is stored, as well as destroy the object on which it is poured."

Criticism hurts. Instead of criticizing someone, it is best to quietly in private tell them. People who lash out at others, without giving a thought about saying something that might hurt, are hurting themselves.

Just as we cannot judge nature, we should not be quick to judge others, for we can't see the motives and intentions in their minds.

Watching what and how you say things between employees, friends and loved ones, can go a long way toward smoothing ruffled feelings.

I had a guest drop a goblet from my expensive stemware that couldn't be replaced. I had to count ten and hardly could control my emotions. I wanted to shout—

CRITICISM HARD TO TAKE

"you clumsy fool!" Instead I carefully picked up the broken pieces and shrugged it off, saying nothing. A week passed and by special delivery mail, from one of the department stores, a box arrived with a sweet note apologizing about the goblet. Amidst all the tissue was a beautiful large cut glass,crystal bowl.

If I had called my guest names, I would have lost a friend. Words in anger sometimes can't be taken back. Control is hard, but necessary. In thinking it out, her friendship was worth more than the goblet.

Many, many years ago, I still remember hurt feelings when my husband made a passing comment about me hanging another of my paintings on our walls. He implied that people coming into the house were obliged to compliment me. He thought I hadn't arrived yet.

I was offended and never said another word, but started to remove them. My eleven year old son stopped me saying, "don't take them down, it makes the house look pretty."

As years passed and I was the recipient of several art awards, Sam couldn't brag enough. When he asked for a painting for his office, I answered, my tone sarcastic, "Have to think about it, don't want to appear like I'm showing off." He looked at me with a surprised expression, which indicated that he really wasn't aware how his disapproving remarks hurt. He learned later, for I made him ask more than once. I finally broke down and then only parted with two. I knew it didn't do me emotionally any good holding anger, because my husband didn't stop and think before he spoke.

STAY YOUNG TO 100

My friend, a special, wonderful man who I became acquainted with when I was one of the Commissioners for the Rockford Park District in Illinois, was the Executive Director for over thirty-five years. He related a story that fits in how people need to— "better bite their tongue than eat their words."

He was only seven years old, the year was 1940, on 4th of July. There was a big celebration at the local airfield. As a child he was intrigued by airplanes. During the celebration he became enthralled with people taking five minute plane rides for 50 cents a ride. Longing for a ride not able to afford it, he just stood by the man selling tickets and watched the people having fun.

Looking down at the little boy the man said, "Sonny, as much as your ears stick out, all you would need are a couple of broom sticks and you could fly without a plane ride."

That statement became a significant emotional occurrence in his life. Till that moment, he never was aware how his ears protruded. From that day, it was on his mind, especially when meeting new people, appearing in groups, or later in life when he made public presentations.

Years passed, and at the age of 55, almost fifty years later, he had corrective surgery on his ears. As my friend says, "What an emotional relief! The surgery proved to be one of the best investments ever made, giving confidence and peace of mind." But his emotional experience still lingered, that ticket salesperson uttering those harsh words, giving no thought how it played on the psyche of this small child, until he was able to do something. The words still linger to this day.

CRITICISM HARD TO TAKE

There are two kinds of criticism: the gentle, tactful, constructive kind which, we all seem to get; and the harsh, blunt kind that hits you in the pit of your stomach. If you're a sensitive person, it is hard to pretend that the words don't hurt. The key is try to force yourself to be dispassionate— it's not easy, but help yourself by thinking who said it, not putting that much importance on it.

The tactful criticism, gentle kind we all get, when we don't even ask we can shrug off. It's the harsh kind that has no purpose but is so hurtful. If possible, you must turn a deaf ear.

When it comes to criticism, most of us don't think about the other person's feelings. Communication skills can help to create a pleasant atmosphere, without causing anger or hurt feelings.

As Disraeli once remarked, *"it is much easier to be critical than correct,"* so there will always be plenty of critics in the world. You can defend yourself against the unkind ones by learning to control your emotional reactions, by adapting a calm attitude.

Do you remember as a child hearing and saying: "Sticks and stones can hurt my bones, but names will never harm me." With that my tongue stuck out at the person who called me names.

Beside criticism there are those young and old who like to gossip. They feed on it. They set a rumor without facts and it spreads like wild-fire. Every day, someone's character is smeared, demeaned. Until proven wrong, the innocent, and his positive qualities, is left damaged.

Emotional control and thinking, is the core. We can learn to respect each other, and realize how we all experience the same hurts reacting to various degrees some less, some more.

As parents, sometimes we have a tendency to criticize our children thinking it is constructive, when in fact, it might be that we have had a hard day dealing with a grabby customer, a boss that was critical of a report, and didn't mince words, harshly criticizing you in front of others. So coming home overtired, stressed out, without thinking, finding fault wasn't constructive, but harsh. Criticism is a direct attack on your self-esteem, so naturally you react with resentment and anger, which makes you more vulnerable.

People who aren't pleased with either themselves, or displeased how life is treating them, find fault striking out to others. This type should take boxing up and spar with someone, physically taking out their mental aggression, and dissatisfaction where it belongs.

No one can hurt you if you don't let them. No one can make you feel less confident, less reliable, less, dependable— if don't you let them. You can develop mental attitudes that become your armor, your shield. Fear, revenge, and hate destroy the body— Lighten up! You will live longer. Healthy is now increasing the way doctors think. Years back doctors only depended on medicine.

When grown up, it boils down to nurturing yourself. Doing things that before you never gave time too. Forget the yard work, do what you want to do. Maybe just curling up reading that book you promised to start. Healthy, vital and alive is what and how you should think. If you have prolonged anxiety, worry, anger, the pressures of today living, will bring on changes in heart, kidney, and other vital organs.

Today doctors recognize that man is a whole unit—body, mind and spirit - each dependant on the other. If one of these factors are not working well it reflects and weakens the other systems. Living a healthy lifestyle, the most important thing, is stop yourself thinking unhealthy, negative thoughts—resentment, hate, anger can't be good for you, it eats into your spirit and drains your energy. As anger brings on stress—stress brings on aging, if you live long enough to tell the tale. It's that small tiny word sometimes that triggers an argument between you and your partner.

"What is wrong with you, can't you do anything right?!" Wow! Those are negative, fighting words.

Keep in harmony with your body. Make it a daily ritual to think healthy and practice healthy. Talk it out and think calmly—analyze your anger, your resentments. The rewards will be positive. Your mind is everything.

It is important to find time to calmly sit and discuss what each want from the other. In long relationships there is a tendency to take the other for granted. The more each tries to accommodate the other's needs, the harder it is to come out of it with less stress.

A recent study revealed that the hormone *cortisol,* which is released into the bloodstream when people feel anxious, can temporarily interfere with memory and rational thinking. Your stressed-out brain trying to get your point of view across will not be clear for better understanding. Be calm and your brain will cool down and you than will be able to collect your thoughts and better express feelings. Fear is the deterrent, a restraint to your mental picture. Say what you want to say—don't let yourself get side tracked.

"The greatest remedy for anger is delay."

If someone in your household has changed from nice to mean, find out what's hurting them. If they seemed change after some accident, it might be that the area in the brain, the "amygdale." This small almond shape mass on the left side of the brain is associated with strong emotions and fear. The more studies are made into the substrata of behavior, the more difficult it becomes to understand.

Dr. Norman Anderson, CEO of the American Psychological Association, talked about latest studies exploring how feelings effect health.

He says faith, and love of friends and family help bring about contentment with your place in life, optimism, openness about your emotions. These positive qualities not only enhance life but also prolong it.

CHAPTER 30

Emotional Control

"Ride your emotions as the boat rides the waves."

Mary Austin

Questions are asked, "What does it means to be human"? How we think out our problems, keep in mind about the impact of "attitude." It is more important than what other people think, or say, or do. It is more important than appearance, than giftedness, or skill. We alone have the choice of what attitude we take on for the day to help us get through trying moments.

I bring up the word self-esteem again, because it's more than just a psychological need during these economic challenging times. Skills that were enough in the past, getting a job, are no longer. It takes more confidence in your own mind thinking through all new demands.

Remember that being overwhelmed is a state of mind. By staying calm thinking through the new demands on your consciousness, no matter your situation is, it is for you to set your priorities and decide what is possible and you make the choices.

EMOTIONAL CONTROL

We all feel overwhelmed and confronted by constant change. In these swift moving times, when everything is so electrically modern and we're all trying to keep ahead of it. This is a big challenge. It can be overwhelming.

I mention the word "Fear" again because it takes over when facing new situations. Keep your mental strength to rationalize and find another avenue. Nothing is final, where one door closes another is waiting for you, use your creative self to open it. Focus on what are the first things that have to be done. Is it taking classes to the new demands for a better job—an increase in salary? Don't frustrate yourself, think calmly and gather your strength. If you have someone in your life to discuss this with, that helps. If not speak it out loud, what must be done. Write down your thoughts, often times it helps seeing what are some priorities.

You are the one to call upon your mental powers, being consciously keen ask, what choices will in the long run alleviate some of the pressures. Being flexible gives you room to cope with every day changes. Avoiding extremes, going far beyond what is reasonable in your thinking.

Adjusting like the Chameleon lizard to the conditions will help you to survive. The important thing to remember is not being rigid.

Five Components of Emotional Intelligence at Work:

Self awareness is the first component of emotional intelligence which makes sense when one considers "know thyself" was spoken as words of wisdom as far back as thousands of years ago. The ability to recognize, understand your moods, emotions, and drives, as well as their effects on others.

Self Regulation is the ability to control or redirect moods and impulses and moods to think before acting. Toughness, intelligence, determination, and vision are required for success.

The most effective leaders are alike in one very important way, they all have a high degree of what is often, times mentioned and that is:

Emotionally intelligent people have mastered their emotions are able to roll with the changes.

Self awareness means having a deep understanding one's emotions, weakness, strengths, needs and drives.

People with strong-awareness are rather honest with themselves and with others. People who have a high degree of self-awareness recognize how their feelings affect other people and their job performance. I might add they will admit to failure and have a sense of humor, being self-deprecating at times when relating a story that pertains to themselves.

Empathy, of all the dimensions of emotional intelligence, empathy is the most easily recognized. Empathy means being intuitively thoughtful, considering others feelings on the job.

Speaking about change, networking is important because the better jobs are less likely to be advertised. That comes under the heading of Social Skills, which is the ability to find common ground and build rapport.

Change doesn't necessarily have to do always with a job, but change is healthy if you think positive and constructively. If you have been doing the same things for the past five years —you're in a rut! You can get depressed when the family all grown, out of the house, the retirement just around the corner you think—now what?

The story was related to me about this spirited woman still going strong, as an attorney doing pro bono legal work. At 60, after retiring from nursing and raising four sons, she decided going back to school and taking a law course, encouraged by one of her sons, a lawyer. She didn't feel intimidated as the professors were young enough to be her sons or grandsons.

With her terrific attitude, today at age 82, still vibrant, when most people her age are content just to watch television, she still enjoys volunteering, which is an added bonus. Her chances for staying young to 100, seem a guarantee. With a great attitude, she stayed in the main stream of life, having so many young friends that keep her mind alert and body healthy, all an added plus. Remember age is only a number.

I have to say by adding her knowledge and experience, being courageous at her age, doing what few would undertake; has given her a healthy long life. Having vision helps— being flexible helps.

Vision is the ability to anticipate possible future events and developments. It is having a far sightedness giving thought, projecting ahead. She had this and did something about the future for her life.

To grow old and wait for the inevitable to happen should not be in anyone's plans. If you wish to grow old fast, take that negative approach, adding years, which is foreseeable.

STAY YOUNG TO 100

Have a vision, follow your dreams, and you will stay young in spirit and health. Every once in awhile pause, ask yourself if you're still on track. Part of being happy is knowing how to live with people the way they are, and with yourself the way you are.

We are trapped in consciousness, trapped by mortality, trapped inside our body, trapped within the poor limitations of the human spirit. Some of us also happen to be caught in smaller prisons within the larger ones, like a mouse in a trap.

If one matures, there are certain drives such as truth, love, pleasure, power, self-esteem, that are necessary for the process of growth, and progress to maturity. Studies have been made where older people get along better with others than younger people do and also are more likely to avoid conflict by just waiting it out. Younger people are impatient, and are more likely to engage in shouting and name-calling.

Perhaps with age one has learned many small lessons of life that patience has its rewards. The New York Times just came out this 2009, that 80% of women are over 100. It could be they're much too smart to waste their energy. There's a new thought giving thanks can be good for your health. Research tells us that people who write in a journal to read over when you're down and blue. Things they're grateful for see things in different ways.

Be thankful, you woke to a new day. Think of even small things that made you feel grateful during the week. Hold that thought and begin this day showing your family with love and gratitude. Make them know your feelings. Be open with your love, with your praise.

EMOTIONAL CONTROL

Make quality time with your guy. With your busy schedule and his, there isn't much time for each other. Be careful that you don't become strangers.

Successful people don't sit around and wait for someone to give them a break; they go after it and work for what they want. People who have self-discipline and a willingness don't try to avoid hard work, they welcome it. Three important principles: having self-discipline, following through being committed.

The successful people nine out of ten times, the way they treat others is a major factor getting ahead. The difference between people who succeed, and those that don't, it really isn't how many times one fails, but the ability to do something after they fail.

George Bernard Shaw once wrote, "I want to be thoroughly used up when I die, for the harder I work, the more I live."

Today, as people live longer, healthier lives, more are delaying retirement. For one, their ability and experience is invaluable to any workplace. Older workers bring more knowledge, experience and reliability. For the woman past having babies, their commitment to the job has a positive response. Regardless of age having a choice being able to work longer into so called, retirement age, some of you are thinking and going into business for self. Others changing careers, and many just remain on their original job that they have been for decades. Workers over 50, companies realize that mature workers have much needed skills and experience and that employing them makes good business sense. The goal is to bring companies and people looking for a job and to promote older workers.

STAY YOUNG TO 100

A study recently made showed that older workers offer positive traits like reliability, loyalty and skills. As older Americans stay on the job, the trend is going in the right direction. It helps to keep working— it gives one purpose, one takes care of self, maintaining health, being well groomed. Besides a continuation of income so don't be so quick to stop working it has many benefits besides the money.

In 1996 just 11.6 percent of Americans over age 65 worked. By 2014 our country will need 900,000 engineers and 3.5 million new teachers, trainers and researchers. There are challenges as technology changes. Every significant change that affects our lives is a challenge to our ability to adapt to all the unfamiliar. The answer is to develop more confidence in your own mind and your competence to cope with life.

CHAPTER 31

What Makes a Winner

"In most things success depends on knowing how long it takes to succeed."

Montesquieu

You all remember the entertainer Tony Bennett, still singing at 87. His zest for life is well known. On his off days he finds time besides recording, he's busy with painting and exhibits. He says, "Always follow your passion, your heart, your dream. Don't say something is impossible." When asked about retiring, his answer is "no, I have too much to learn yet." With that attitude, he will remain healthy, forever young in the main stream of life.

The examples of people who have managed to overcome difficulties and progressed making their lives worthwhile is to take note. None made excuses for themselves whether having a handicap, or coming up the ladder the hard way. They had a purpose— a goal.

When his older brother was killed during World War Two, he first withdrew into a shell. He lost touch with the world and stayed indoors listening to the radio to ease the pain. He began starting to dream about hosting his own radio show.

That man, Dick Clark started American Bandstand. Those people are all winners. There's a distinguishing feature in being a winner than a loser:

A winner: tries to judge his own acts by their consequences and other people's acts by their intentions; a loser gives himself all the best of it by judging his own acts by his intentions, and the acts of others by their consequences:

A winner: feels that his past failures have contributed to his success; a loser feels that his past failures blocked his success.

A winner: rebukes and forgives; a loser is too timid to rebuke and too petty to forgive.

A winner: accepts the fact that finally; no mortal can know who the real winners or losers are.

We all share a common destiny. All living substances of being, share the same destiny. All those people we love, and those we know little of, are united and share the same—we are born and die and share this unity. We share the sun, the earth, strangers the flowers in the fields.

You must have faith to accept the mystery and build upon strength and realize that some things never change— children's laughter, the glory of the stars, the innocence of morning, the wonderment of spring with all its fresh new buds, ready to burst forth to another season.

With each new day, you must wake with the thought that the bad situations you leave behind. Today is a new vision of awareness realizing that only you can live a fuller, better more healthful today and tomorrow, because you have set your choices on the positive.

Coping with life is a challenge, no one will deny it. But having said this, we move on and reach out to find happiness with as little stress as possible.

Your mind is everything, keep using it with positive thoughts. Stress makes us look and feel old. Staying young while growing old is living life to the fullest, stepping out of the comfort zone and not being afraid to take chances.

Setting goals help us, take charge of our lives. It helps to better understand what is possible. "Goals," build confidence—goals are setting a standard, aiming and working toward something—things that you want to do. "Wishes," are not goals—wishes are vague—unthinking in the mind.

Things that you want to achieve - define write them down. Things that you want to learn to better your career. Set goals in each area, what and who can help to further your goals. Refer to your list, from time to time, less you forget what you have set your sights on achieving. Do not fall into a rut, but keep active will keep you full of energy while reaching 100.

Timing is very important. One financial consultant says, don't ask for a raise the first thing on Monday or Friday. Those two days the boss is in no mood to listen to reasons why you should get that raise due you. And also, the first of the week people are busy making up what they didn't take care of on Friday. Friday, your supervisor will be hurrying to finish and be off.

Some tips for setting your goals are how to manage your life better. With better timing your days will be enriched. Something to think about when asking for a raise when you deserve it. The best time is right after lunch or early in the morning on Wednesday or Thursday. Of course come prepared, letting it be known what you're interests are in the company and what you bring to the job.

Allocating and figuring your time, you can't put a price on it, something you won't tax your system and feel less pressured, which helps your nervous system, which keeps your blood pressure normal. Proper timing gives quality to your life.

If you're thinking of buying a new car, usually auto prices are better negotiable at the end of every month. Salespersons are more flexible.

Living consciously, go after it with all that you are, knowing that life will meet you halfway. Anytime you learn something new about yourself or about life, you have progressed.

In a recent study, one researcher found that athletes, whose teammates were in a good mood, were more likely to feel happy themselves. Outward signs of bliss are hard to disguise. Though there can be no name for it, I have called it the, "way of life."

Perhaps, I should have called it "the fullness of life." Since fullness implies widening into space—still further widening. Implies widening until the circle is whole. In this sense:

The way of life is fulfilled, Heaven is fulfilled, and a fit person also is fulfilled. There are four amplitudes of the universe and a fit person is one of them:

People, rounding the way of earth, earth rounding the way of heaven, heaven rounding the way of life, till the circle is full.

The person who is at peace with themselves is one that is happy, healthy and successful.

CHAPTER 32

Never Think Defeat

"Failure is never fatal, it's courage that counts."

Sir Winston Churchill

Defeat denotes failure. Words often times motivate how we act upon a situation. Life can be overwhelming sometimes. It can almost defeat us, providing we let us be defeated. Do you lay down and be defeated? That's giving up. "Never accept defeat." With defeat comes "self pity."

Stop feeling sorry for yourself. Stop saying, "why me?" I went through that when my son was killed. When I stopped to find answers and act upon the knowledge, that turned my life around. It was an emotional relief almost like a weight lifted off my back finding simply rational answers.

Never think defeat, but how do I handle the present situation that I'm in? You will change your thinking, what you accept in your mind. And now, you can begin to think, with a plan to move away from defeat.

You change your thinking "I will fill my mind with… "I won't be defeated and will come out of this bad situation." Talking to self really helps one.

NEVER THINK DEFEAT

Keep thinking victory, hope, and believing. The test of one's character is how tenacious they are. Stay with the positive thought, never give in—never give up!

The attitude to take is persistence. No road block will stop you. You never know how close you are to succeeding. It could be just one moment away— a day away. You be a fighter hang on—hang in there!

Sir Winston Churchill, will be remembered for his great leadership during the second world war, helped the English people get through most difficult times with his speeches, and courageous leadership.

Never did he think of defeat. He would repeat, "tomorrow will be better; the day will come when we will win. The final victory will be ours!"

Fear and worry go hand in hand. With some people it's a habit that they can't seem to break. Guess there are a lot of things to worry about today. Most things that we all worry about never happen, so why waste your time thinking about them?

If you do not control your thoughts, you will find those creases called, frown lines deepen. Getting the best out of life requires firstly, being logical, "Should" is a good word to hang onto.

We break down our systems by worry, stress, fear, negative thinking. We are victims of our own thoughts. The older we get we must reinforce our system with healthy thoughts and actions. These keep us young while growing old. I'll repeat, "The mind is everything" you can't solve anything if the mind is hot—agitated. Keep cool.

STAY YOUNG TO 100

When in our teens, we conducted our lives with wanting immediate gratification. If it didn't happen we did foolish things, taking the wrong road many a times. That's foolish thinking. Growing older, we understand that isn't how the world operates to succeed.

With each new day there are life lessons, how to keep your mind sharp and changing from negative thinking to positive. If you don't like where you're at in your relationship, your job, or your finances—stop being depressed, take control. You have choices— change the mix.

"Defeat is nothing but education; the first step to something better."

Wendell Phillips

I spoke of goals. It helps being guided by a vision and shoot for it. Doing something will take the worry out of it. Thinking calmly, constructively your mind will come to a decision. Human beings go through repeated sequences of events repeated again and again. Discouragement has much to do with mood changes from high to low—good and bad. Those feelings of loss of motivation, confidence, worry, are part of mood swings.

The loss of motivation makes it hard to start a new day. Look around you is there anything that you are to be grateful for? Welcome this new day, filled with optimism—hope.

Discouragement is formed by the pretax "dis"— before courage. A philosophical doctrine purposed by

Leibnitz, that belief in the Power of Good. The belief that things are continually getting better and good will triumph over evil. There is much truth obtaining the compassionate state of mind. Giving of oneself for a cause makes life more purposeful. Sharing is one of the first lessons a parent can teach their child.

Humans are hoarders. They like to keep buying and they stash away "stuff" it makes them happy with possessions, but does it? We are always searching for more "stuff." It fills a void. It isn't some trophy that we earned. It is an emotional cover-up making us for the moment feeling good. Get to the root of your mood swings. "Why?" People are motivated by their moods. Some have dramatic mood swings.

"Control, attitude, choice, courage, should"— aren't just words idly cast upon a page, but words to make an impression on your brain as to what actions to take to help overcome your mood changes.

Try and keep basic set of principles—concepts as for truth, ethical standards—things that always can be relied upon and yes, maintaining courage, deep within your thoughts. You will find that discouragement fades. You will find that mood changes fade.

Work on a set of principles, if you take control you will have less mood changes and be less discouraged, which is pulling you down and not helping you think clearly and wisely. The sooner you discover what is troubling your mind—only with honesty with self, the sooner you will understand how to change a bad mood into a good one. You will be a happier person, ready to make decisions that will be beneficial, positive, and less discouraging, rewarding for your life. Those mood changes understanding the why and confronting them, they will become less.

Self identity is recognizing that quality unique to you. So the sooner we learn more who we are, we will learn what we want out of life and become less frustrated less unhappy and recognize the steps getting there making us fulfilled.

Anytime you learn something new about yourself or about life, you have progressed.

CHAPTER 33

Sorry, the Super Glue

"Regret is to be sorry and let the other one know."

Anonymous

So much of what we are stems from childhood days, how we were raised with values and honesty. If my parents knew to praise us, they were quick to do so. In fact, in their eyes we could do no wrong, which can backfire. It does have merit when and if you can think of something in your own life where saying "sorry," made a big difference in a relationship.

I might say that it wasn't difficult for me as an adult, when something needed an apology I swallowed my pride and said what needed to be. Men sometimes find it beneath them to back off and admit a wrong. I believe it has to do with something in their childhood that never was taught. We all make mistakes, and there is no shame to admit to it. Even big, strong men can say—"sorry!" It actually helps one eliminate anxiety it builds character. In the end of the day it can bring peace of mind feeling content. Forgiveness goes a long way to mend a broken heart.

SORRY, THE SUPER GLUE

The secret to happiness and well-being— is:

To be able to forget.
To be able to apologies.
To be able to admit errors.
Forgiveness is the sweetest revenge.

As a small child of six, I was shopping with my mother in Marshall Fields, in Chicago (now called Macy's). While she was trying on some shoes, I slowly wandered nearby to the jewelry section.

What caught my eye were the Opal Rings laid out on top of the counter, in all there splendor. By just managing to raise up on my tip-toes, I could see them better. Opal stones have a great variety of different colors that give an incredible amount of sparkle, which fascinated me.

Reaching up I touched one— I touched another. They were all so beautiful, I was fascinated. Never giving another thought, I took one, and slipped it into my pocket. Every little while, I'd take a peek without my mother being aware of what I clutched tightly in my hand in my pocket.

That same evening, as I undressed for bed, I held the opal ring, slowly turning it in the palm of my hand admiring how the fiery colors seem to speak to me, but something inside of me felt uneasy. I was afraid my mother would be very angry with me. I didn't want her to know I had the ring and looked around my room for a place to hide it. My eyes rested on my dresser. I tucked it under my pajamas. During the week, I would slowly take the ring from the drawer and just kept admiring it. I was fascinated with the brilliant colors.

One day, while playing outdoors, I heard my mother's voice calling. "Charlotte I have to see you now!" Her voice rang sharp and clear. As I entered my bedroom, there she stood near the open dresser drawer with her outstretched hand holding the ring.

"Where did you get this ring?" She asked, frowning hard at me. "I took it," I replied. "You took it from where?"

"From that big store" I said. She never said another word, but left the room shaking her head from side to side, looking back at me frowning.

That Saturday, we went downtown to the store where upon my mother, asked to see the manager of the jewelry department. As we waited for him, my mother handed the ring to me, and looked deep in my eyes, it seemed to send a message.

I remember being very scared as I held the ring in the palm of my hand. As the manager approached, tears slowly filling my eyes, I stuck out my hand and said, "I'm sorry, I took this ring, I'm giving it back."

"I don't understand," he said side glancing at my mother, than back at me. I repeated, "I took it, it doesn't belong to me!" I hardly could get the words out. I still can remember the expression on his face—puzzled and pleased that my mother was about to teach her child right from bad actions.

My mother never said another word going home, but her silence was enough to make a lasting memory of a childish happening that I learned from. I had broken her trust.

Days passed, there was praise and compliments for my other sisters and brother, but nothing for me. It seemed I was excluded, with any discussion, ignored as if I didn't belong to this family. The usual thing, tucking me in at night— stopped.

I wished I had never taken that ring and realized what a bad thing I did. She punished me in her own way by ignoring me most of the time. It was worse than if she had spanked me.

One day she found me crying in my room. As she gathered me in her arms, drying my tears, I mumbled under my breath, "You don't love me anymore." She kissed me tenderly and said something to the effect that— "taking something that didn't belong to me was dishonest" I looked at her. "I'm sorry I took the ring, will you ever love me?" The fact I learned an important lesson, that I felt badly—"yes" she said, "I still love you!"

The incident stayed deep in my mind forever. I learned that I did something wrong, and losing her respect mattered. Mom hugged me and my world felt right once again.

It was once said that apology is the superglue of life. It can repair guilt. It is ultimately your decision, your choice, your attitude, which will reap the benefits, for a better approach to a healthier longer life. The rewards for positive thoughts and actions can help to "stay young while growing old." Apology is an admission of guilt and for those who find it almost impossible to say sorry, it is admitting firstly something was done wrong. Once over that thought, it becomes less difficult.

My husband found it very hard to say sorry. His apology came in a different act more like a hug, a kiss, a look that said "forgive me for being stupid." Living so long with a person who finds it hard to say, "sorry," still hurts. If I asked, "are you sorry?" He might say "Yes!" He knew I was bugged that he couldn't say the words that I almost had to force it out of him.

When we lived out West, I remember we had a squabble over something I can't remember what, but I was hurt enough to get into the car late at night and drive out to the Reservation where I sat and cried, and debated whether to take the children and leave him. Of course I cooled down and waited for the apology.

I guess Sam finally realized what it took to make amends which was a simply, "I am sorry!" So terribly simple, but so terribly hard for many.

CHAPTER 34

Handling Disappointments

"No man, with a man's heart gets far without some bitter soul-searching, disappointment."

Brown

I can go through a hundred and one things that bring on disappointments, rejections, disapproval damaging to our confidence. Destroying belief in our own abilities. Anticipating a raise that didn't come through, is just one example. These are unhappy, frustrating moments, we have no control over.

It was asked who ought to be the tenor in the quartet; the answer was "it is obvious it should be the man who can sing tenor." Ability is aptitude, skill, talent. One must not lose sight in the belief in our own abilities, trusting and self reliant are ever so important for building the inner peace that keeps us mentally fit. That keeps us courageous, permitting us to go forth and venture once again with new energy, optimism and renewed vision.

The outcome of going through disappointments is fear, tension, stress, which pulls one down mentally and physically. Being depressed keeps you in a low mood and if it lingers over the weeks, one should take themselves to a doctor who understands physiological problems and can help get you back on track.

With all this stress, one can actually see tell-tale ageing lines around the face. How to cope? How to learn from our mistakes? How to be wise? Knowing that you're not alone is little comfort. Mentally reprimanding yourself doesn't find answers.

Simple suggestions for warding off depression; diversion is a major step. Exercising, being with friends — a good support system. Don't sit around and dwell on what you should have done. Think calmly and your mind will find the proper answers to pull you through the difficult moments.

Tomorrow is another day. Reflect on what you have and be thankful. Go forth with courage, not thinking negative.

When studies have been made about people having longevity, all seem to have good balance to their thinking. "They don't dwell on what was."

Acting on the thought counts…just the thought doesn't count.

Remember Grandma Moses who didn't dwell on all her difficult times, but pushed them aside and did something positive instead?

Mychal Wynn wrote a wonderful saying, I'll mention a few lines:

DARE: to encounter obstacles when all around you avoid conflict;

DARE: to remain strong when all around you are weakening;

DARE: to have faith when all around you doubt;

DARE: to seek possibilities when all around you see only the impossible;

DARE: to dream even if no one dreams with you.

Though I am no longer a Park Commissioner, I receive monthly a magazine, "Parks and Recreation." One article by Sandy Kimbrough, Ph.D found me agreeing. Efficacy is important through play. The Park offers so many sports to the young and old.

People that camp, do rock-climbing, hiking, boating—have extended pay backs from enjoying the outdoor benefits. Those that enjoy the outdoors will tell you that it provides a benefit to their mental and emotional health: They feel refreshed, energized and like that they "escaped" the pressures of their every-day lives.

Researchers have looked into the relationship between structured outdoor recreational experiences and changes in the affective self-efficacy.

The meaning of efficacy is the belief in one's ability to accomplish something. It is the individual's judgment, of his or her capabilities to complete courses of action and is related to self-esteem and self-concept.

Self-efficacy looks on optimistic, self belief that one can perform a novel or difficult task or cope with adversity in various areas of human functions. People believe that they are capable and that they can handle circumstances that happen around them.

The article was written and featured in the magazine to examine the relationship between self-efficacy, and participation in outdoor recreational activities. Outdoor recreational activities contribute to their overall well-being. One of the philosophies of outdoor sports, "toughens up"— those and develops a greater ability to deal with real-world challenges.

I still carry a card that states the *Mission and Purpose of our Parks and what they offer:*

To help its citizens enjoy life by providing a quality park and recreational system: Residents value recreation as essential for a healthy life: Residents are involved in diverse and well-supported recreational activities for their health, well-being and entertainment.

The physical and emotional and over-all well being is a big factor making the study so valuable. A group of young people who participated in a wilderness, orientation program they observed in perceived competence 8 weeks of modest gains, after the completion of the group trip. Students were asked to write about their experience. The response was positive. Firstly, much was learned of self.

It is a known factor, that exercise in a variety of subjects can only be positive, both in body and spirit and helps ward off stress and maintains with good health, confidence and life expectance is increased.

There are moments that all of us question what went wrong. When we finished high school and went off to College and thought we had a great job waiting using what we learned— success eluded. We wondered, what went wrong—why?

Sights set high, you keep at it, you seem to get your toe in the door but somehow the door never fully opens. We wonder why? With the passing of a few years, it becomes a discouraging journey. You are losing hope feeling there's nothing to look forward too.

The answer is courage, don't give up! We never know what is just around the corner— just a turn in the road; a storm one day, the next day, the clouds part and the sun shines down bright.

There was a young man in high school who failed every subject. Throughout his youth, he didn't do well socially. He was a loser in everything, but one— Sparky loved to draw. Specifically, he loved to draw funny cartoons that no one particularly cared for, but he was convinced that he had talent and so pursued an art career, and decided to become a professional artist. After completing high school, he wrote a letter to the Walt Disney Studios, and upon request, submitted some samples of his drawings he was rejected— another loss.

So Sparky decided to write his autobiography all in cartoons. He described his early childhood as a looser and an under-achiever.

This under-achiever, this boy loser, was Charles Schultz, who created the "Peanuts" comic strip and the cartoon character, Charlie Brown.

"If you can conceive it and believe it you can achieve it."

Napoleon Hill

"Many of life's failures are people who did not realize how close they were to success when they gave up."

Thomas Edison

HANDLING DISAPPOINTMENTS

All through ones life we are faced with stumbling blocks that make it difficult to pursue our goals. It takes powers of positive thought along the way with courage and determination to make stumbling blocks into stepping stones.

Understanding a little more each day—not to try is to risk failure. To try gives you hope, strength, courage. Don't forget some of the important information, one to keep in mind: only you can make choices, keeping you happy, and healthy, a little wiser— coping and better understanding your fears, worries, tension; and how important attitude is.

The healthy attitude is having confidence, accepting, how do you like yourself and see you facing life's challenges— worthy, commendable.

Don't hesitate to sometimes reach out to another worrying that there is the possibility of involvement: Crying to express emotion—to express deep feelings, and risk appearing sentimental. To let your feelings be known that dreams are important.

Hold onto—"try" that tiny word that has so many big possibilities. To sometimes go out on that shaky limb, not be afraid to take challenges. To know that the greatest hazard in life is risking nothing… one who risks nothing— does nothing, will never be free.

CHAPTER 35

You Become What You think

"A long life is a blessing of God. But a happy life is our own doing."

Anonymous

Keep the thought you are constantly in a state of becoming, and you become what you think. You have within you considerable potential. It takes courage and strength to help over the difficult problems, which when you accept are part of life.

Stop for a moment and reflect upon your week. Did you make a conscientious effort to improve your working place, your home place at this moment with a new attitude, a deeper understanding of self?

Man keeps asking to understand life better—handle it better and be more alive in their response to it. There are many obstacles that interfere with our abilities. That's where knowing, who we are helps overcome much.

Not only making more discoveries, knowing to like ourselves, patience reassess where the new person has emerged will come forth; over time, grown in dimension, learning the smallest assets, where with all. It will happen.

YOU BECOME WHAT YOU THINK

Like the caterpillar breaking out of its cocoon, opening and moving on to a new way of life.

Humans go through many stages until they are finally complete. Like the force of nature that we are, we go from a bud to a materialization of adulthood, to the slowly down time with retirement, to honor what you always wanted to do. Remember never stop living life to its fullest, no matter what the hour of your life.

Life becomes easier if we understand, we can help solve some of our pressing problems if we can shed the burden of the past and let our vision of what we want for the future guide us. The more emotionally healthy a person is, the better he has reasonable self-confidence to see him through the bad times, and the experiences of being rejected.

Human beings can do amazing things under all conditions. Most never tap into what they can do because they put too much on self limitations. Your mind, if not restricted, the hidden resources will come forth. If you wish to make more of yourself—stay focused on what you want.

What you want means not giving up. If asked "are you a courageous person?" You probably would answer no! Your mind construes, quickly rescuing someone from a burning building. That is not necessarily what courageous is about.

Actually we all are courageous. At some point in our life, when we are able to meet the challenges and accept when faced with handling disappointments, we have been courageous. With the loss of a love one we have been courageous. Having inner strength, keeping oneself thinking, emotionally calm is an act of courage—of being brave. When we have shown self-awareness strength of mental endurance, having a deep understanding of one's emotions— we are courageous.

Those who have a high degree of self-awareness recognize their feelings and others. People who have mastered their emotions are able to roll with adversity.

It takes a degree of boldness as it tells the mind not to hesitate and it sets a pattern to go forth and do something filling your potential. Fear is the obstacle that holds you back. The unknown always carries fear. Stop and analyze, if you have a creative thought follow through with it.

If you subdue the fear you clear the way and now have control. Remember the mind stretches and can do impossible things. Achieving what you want out of life means self-discipline—doing what it takes.

Self-discipline is the capability to do what you should be doing. Not some of the time, but every day. It is reaching out when overwhelmed, and staying positive and productive with a purpose. It is managing emotion under pressure, accomplishing what you want.

Keep reflecting on these paragraphs. You will be able to understand what only you can do to make, your life better lived. Preaching is not my intent, calling attention to facts, what can make you stay healthy in body and mind is what I am trying to get across. With the right message hopefully one can stay young to 100.

Like climbing the highest mountain, take one step forward at a time. Resting a moment, with one thought — achieving your goal with positive results getting where you want to be. It is with full purpose that life becomes significant. Our existence, how we keep maintaining proper mental input. There is no need to be bored, life can be packed full of meaning.

Live one day at a time and make it a masterpiece.

There are two ways to conduct your thinking. It is reasonable, logical, and positive. With strength of mind, a new head set, having the tools to make you think calmly. You will be less stressed, healthier and have the spirit of young at heart. Staying young while growing old: takes mind over matter, takes attitude, takes honesty, takes acknowledging love with friends and family— giving and receiving—takes making choices. You have much more than a lot of others, when you never lose hope, and are answerable. Patience means keeping your emotions in check.

Giving, not only with the dollar, but to give of self, in services is mentally rewarding. Reaching out to help others is as fundamental as communication. All humans are endowed with compassion.

Remember to give. Seek it out in your marriage and family, it will bring contentment. People, who don't give, aren't ahead in feeling good. People who don't give are self centered, selfish and seldom win. They are the takers.

To foster health, vigor, energy, keep thinking what makes you healthier. For one day, don't hold anger. For one day, speak no resentment. For one day, no negative thoughts. Try it! It will change your attitude.

The results will be so rewarding giving you, that extra bounce in your step. You will be smiling often at your family, your co-workers. You will have the power within—you will be in control.

Now is the only time that really exists. Your spirit will soar. You will smile more and look and feel years younger!

The other week, I walked around most of the day with the zipper on my blue jeans open. I was so embarrassed, I wanted to run around apologizing to the world how silly I felt. When I mentioned it to a co-worker she said, "I never noticed anything!"

"She never noticed anything?" Guess it proves people are absorbed with themselves. We all have been klutzes at some time.

From Cornel College, the prominent psychologist, Thomas Gilovich, did various studies with several teams of students doing various acts, wanting to know the opinions and reactions of others. The reason may be that at one time, all of us have done stupid things, like forgetting to zip our flies, tripping on the sidewalk, and 80 percent have spilled water on their pants looking like they wet themselves.

In these difficult times, it is more important to reflect on what really matters. As you have only one life to live, it is more important how you make each moment count, as tomorrow isn't a promise, treasure each minute.

How you think is vital to your health. It isn't impossible to think yourself sick. *You are what your think.* Emotional stress could produce depression.

The willingness to make conscious choices is another way of demonstrating, that you are ready to find new ways of living. When what we do, how we do it and the way we do it, no longer fits our purpose in life, we must choose to do something else. That is reasonable thinking.

This means we are aware of our patterns and dissatisfied, we no longer accept them. This is called choice. We no longer are in a hold pattern, but realizing the power within, when we decide consciously to choose a new and different path we become courageous and drop our fears.

We are in control. Most times, what we imagine is far worse than the truth. To know truth, you learn more about you're ability to understand and recognize that making choices isn't set in concrete, if you see a particular choice isn't going so well, you can change your decision and make a more favorable choice.

Choice is my divine teacher.
Silence is a Choice not to choose.
Unconscious Choice wins by default.
What I resist will persist.
Conscious Choice is the path to personal power.

From- "Let Me Remember" Iyanla Vanzant

Reflect upon the words by Iyanla Vanzant. It helps to give you mental guidance to think better in your daily life, helping to live with less stress and more happiness.

If you are experiencing a down mood it will pass and not to let fear grip you and cloud your rational thinking. Breathe deeply, relax your thoughts and realize that the power of the word, gives you power of your thoughts. Thoughts turn to actions.

Let your actions be with thoughts and always know you have choice. You have an inner wise-self—use it! Talk to yourself. Your subconscious mind is constantly at work.

If you can maintain optimism in the face of disappointment visualizing beyond your troubles, you won't stay long in your present state of mind if your mind is sending.

CHAPTER 36

Stay With Attitude

"He who learns the rules of wisdom without conforming to them is like a man who ploughs his field but does not sow."

Saadi

The word "attitude" has such powerful logic to make such a difference in how we think and relate to others and how they think of us, under various circumstances of someone's life. I feel attitude needed mentioning again.

Attitude is a word that keeps us on track and well balanced. It's your conscious assertiveness, a point of view, an opinion.

Attitude is impact on life. It is more important than facts, than money, than circumstances, than the past. You say how can it be? It's all how your attitude is to a situation. If you are mindful, and keep the right attitude that day, that moment, for any situation, you will come out ahead. Harness your true power by maximizing self.

If you are new in a community and want to meet someone, every library has an event listing. Attend a workshop or seminar about a topic of interest that resonates with you.

There's no reason to be lonely, the important thing is, we have a choice, we can do something to help our situation and make ourselves happier, less stressed.

Having accumulated knowledge on human behavior over a long period of years in the field working and observing young and old, has given me experience, a greater insight, observing in what I like to call, "life's teacher." Witnessing what works when positive input is practiced, results from good decisions through good choices has given me the creditability to speak out in hopes that one can learn the do's and don'ts of making life on this planet, better fulfilled and happier.

We get there faster by being less timid, more exuberant, and more courageous. Think about the successful people you know and read about. They all have something in common—tenacity, and firmness of purpose. They never think of failure. When opportunity knocks they are quick to open the door. Positive thinking has positive rewards.

The mind is not easy to understand. It reacts to your thoughts and words. You are in control of your mind. If how you think is hard to change, than it will be. If you can talk to your mind, because you have the power to make choice, and toss those past fears out the window and breathe in fresh thoughts, you will find it easier to make a decision, make the change in your life, and yes better understanding the next one.

Having a plan and setting sights on a goal helps you become successful. Don't stop short and nothing will stop you from achieving results.

Reorganize, alter your thoughts move away from negative feelings and put more attention on what it is that you really do want to be or have. Being too rigid in one's thinking slows you down. Today one can't pick up a magazine without reading something about stress and related problems.

You can stay young to 100: by being active, open to change, being a participant in what's going on round you, and not just passing time and rusting out. You've heard me say age is only a number. While you are alive, you have to feel in control of your life and that you still contribute to society.

You are not imprisoned. Your mind might be worried and over burdened, but while you still breathe the air, and can reason logically, your inner-wise self, will be able to find new ways. Many a time, respond to difficult situations with more patience and less anger, for if you give in to these emotions, you create additional reasons for your own suffering.

Trying to get even, holding on to past hurts, the longer you live, realize the impact that your attitude is more important than what is said, or done to you— whatever the circumstance is, whatever some other person hurtfully says, or does we have a choice everyday regarding the attitude we take.

If confronted stay with that word, "attitude" and let no person pull you down for your positive mind can keep you strong inside of you.

STAY WITH ATTITUDE

Every right attitude can turn a problem into good fortune. And every disadvantage can be changed into an advantage.

Pause and listen to your conscious mind. Be calm and question, what's hindering me from moving forward? Shove those foolish fears aside.

We all worry about things that never happen. To hesitate slows you down. Being undecided stops any decisions. Develop a new attitude for making positive moves.

Since the human being's mind is so complex, it is difficult to understand why people do the things that they do. But one thing to holds true— human beings all seek happiness.

It was asked of the Dalai Lama, "is it a reasonable goal for most of us?" His answer, "Yes, by training the mind, by bringing a certain inner discipline you undergo your entire attitude and approach to living. One important thing is willingness to reach out to others, to create a feeling of goodwill, even in a very brief encounter."

Good health is one factor for a happy life. Good health is a factor for longevity. Another is to have friendships or companions. Your state of mind is extremely important for a feeling of exuberance, maintaining high energy. If you keep your mind open there sometimes is another perspective on how to view another that helps you accept better.

A dear friend of mine, a second grade teacher, told me that she was happier this day, because she was able to change her perspective about a little boy in her class, who was disruptive, impatient, and shouting out answers, not always correct, disrupting the class - a hard one to manage.

Relating her story, I could see in her face how pleased and happy she was. Being a teacher for twenty years, she decided that she would find something about this boy to change her mind about him what to do to curb her anger, and frustration. She was ashamed of these feelings.

She felt that the boy wasn't getting the attention he craved from his home, and was overpowered by six other siblings. He had a personality problem.

This day as she was passing out some papers, little Tommy looked up at her, and for the very first time she actually paused to look in his face— in his eyes, and was surprised how beautiful his round, deep brown eyes, fringed with thick lashes, were.

"Tommy, you have such nice eyes." She said. Those few words were like magic. "I smiled at Tommy and he gave me a nice, big smile back."

From that day my friend concentrated on that small little face with those beautiful eyes. When he started to shout out answers my friend didn't scold him, but put her finger to her lips smiled and nodded.

Tommy knew that she had his attention and he slowly gained confidence. Changing her negative perspective, my friend learned one big lesson.

Changing one's perspective to view one's problems allows one to take on a new viewpoint. The end results will help achieve self awareness and show how changing one's limited perspective it can reduce anger, and cultivate patience. With patience comes tolerance. Developing a flexible approach to living helps us cope with everyday problems and is another key for good balance, and a longer healthier life.

Start each day by seeing it the way you would want it to be. Keep your proper attitude. See yourself each day moving through the day with a smile and joy in your heart. Those around you will respond to your peace and joy. It is important to frame your mind whatever it is— let it be good. I agree it isn't always that easy to recognize your good qualities. Begin each day by telling yourself nice things, positive things. Compliment yourself. Remember to take pride about some accomplishment, the small ones will do too.

It is absolutely necessary to flood your mind with positive thoughts about yourself. It will add years to your life. It will add health to your life. You will stay younger while growing old.

The subconscious mind is so powerful. It keeps track of every word we ever heard. It can remember who spoke to us in anger. The written and spoken word determines what and how we do in life and how we do it.

The poet, Maya Angelou, believes the written and spoken word in our environment soaks into our being and becomes a part of who we are what we do, in life and how we do it—words guide our actions.

Selecting words and actions are important to counteract the unpleasant things that sometimes others speak about us. It is important that we counteract by speaking words of love, truth and every good things that we desire to experience.

If you don't have the right attitude, you are your own worse enemy. "What's wrong with me? I can't seem to get anything right!" All of us have walked around not feeling fulfilled. Feeling that something we wanted didn't happen. Was it, we didn't put enough to a project?" Doubting— "wasn't I good enough?" The belief creates the actual fact. Negative thinking can pull you down can destroy your confidence. It is important to keep the mind free of disbelief.

Finding more hidden powers within yourself, changing negative thoughts, calling upon your strengths rather than concentrating on your weak points is the beginning to move ahead and understand that all the resources for achieving happiness in home or your job, all rests within one person—YOU! Attitude is how you view everything.

Begin each day by seeing it the way you would want to see it. Not seeing results immediately, they will eventually happen. Deepak Chopra says:

"Until you peel away the layers around your soul, you will never realize the clear, timeless core that lies at your center."

"When you discover your essential nature and know who you really are, in that knowing itself, is the ability to fulfill any dream you have."

People have to have compassion, and love. In a thirty-year study of a group of Harvard graduates, researcher George Vaillant, mentioned that altruistic lifestyle is a component of good mental health. Of over 90 percent of volunteers, their responses were one of a kind of euphoria and a feeling of self worth and personal happiness.

STAY WITH ATTITUDE

There is evidence to back up the claims about physical and emotional benefits that developing altruism has impact on emotional health. Having the concern of others is a grand compassionate state of mind.

The difference, or opposite of not having compassion, thinking only of self leads to callousness, brutality, and total indifference. I repeat - these people are selfish, self-centered thinking only in terms of, "what will I get out of it?"

All humans want to avoid suffering and hope to have happiness, it doesn't need to be learned to have it. Yes, there is an art to living: Take one day at a time, don't bother to dwell on the past mistakes, it is a memory. The future is today and it is all the potential you put into it.

Do I sound like a broken record? Well play it again and again.

You can't control how the world conceives you. Unfortunately many of our conceptions of self-worth come about from our early childhood home life. Reflect back on either one of your parents, how did they act and think. How did they act to you? Do you see yourself as a mirror of them? Learn to be a little more patient for if you know what you want is clear in your mind, it should come to you.

Too much of the time, we walk around, not knowing what we want, or too afraid to do what we want. As an adult, the more honest you are, the more self-confident you will be. With it you have courage to help make choice and reach your goal. Try and not take life too seriously.

CHAPTER 37

Gratitude

"You and you alone can control how you wish to be conceived."

Anonymous

Gratitude is another word to ask of yourself. Giving thanks for even the little things that you have been fortunate to experience. Some people never have any of the good things, but live a life stressed, not able to meet daily necessities, caring for a sick parent; a one parent raising children to care for—daily burdens financially overwhelming—separated from a husband.

St Francis of Assisi said, "Start by doing what is necessary, then what's possible and suddenly you're doing the impossible." You and you alone can control your own destiny.

Many of those good acts of self, satisfaction, gives you confidence. Cultivating positive mental views as kindness and compassion leads to better feelings, of worth giving you more to your own abilities. Giving of yourself, to others adds richness to your life.

GRATITUDE

Clear conscience, a healthy mental attitude, a grateful spirit and a heart full of love, this is a big portion to the secret of happiness. As time goes on, you transform your mind to start believing in worth through deeds, than your mind will begin transforming negative mental traits to positive changes. The more good input, thus the idea for training the mind for more confidence—more happiness we gain.

Giving to others improves our self-image. It also turns our focus outward so we're less likely to think only of our problems. You don't have to win the lottery before becoming generous—that may never happen. Generous isn't always money. Giving of services to the community is a big plus.

During the depression, I can remember many a time coming home and seeing my mom feeding several people at our back door. She was there helping out in her own way doing a good deed, which in return made her happy. My father, a doctor, on many occasion, gave his services free to needy families.

By finding a way each day to help someone improve their life, it improves yours. If only giving a helping hand, letting them know that someone can be counted on in time of their need.

Being confronted with problems over a long period we are literally trapped with seeing our way clear. Take time out be wise, calm down. The answer you're looking for to help solve your problems, will happen with thinking in a fresh way, positive, not being totally absorbed the mind is over worked in thinking the same thing making the problem worse.

If we panic, the brain is in a state of dilemma so the best thing is try and stay calm you can't think with a hot mind.

Sound reasoning is another word for logic. If human beings can master and apply to a situation, it can change one's position from hopeless to first thing is "mind over matter," think calmly which takes discipline— helping to maintain emotional balance frees the mind, to solving the problem.

Pay attention to your feelings. Recognizing your feelings come into play solving problems, because when we think we feel our thoughts. If in our thinking, we use little reasoning, our feelings tell us. Being able to have feelings and feeling good, becomes a natural state of mind, so we feel at peace— emotionally we have the problem in hand. Feelings and what you think are connected.

There is another thing, when we feel we become aware of our surroundings and others. How much understanding do you have? If you have understanding, you have tolerance, you are open minded. Your days are happier, for you are able to view others as you would like them, to see you not by the color of your skin, but seeing one who is not judging but acceptance on the merit of another human being.

Being aware and understanding your feelings are very important. They can be a warning signal to not keeping your anger in check and your resentments. Being wise, having control shifting your thoughts back to a healthy, positive right feeling condition—where you want to be, where happy thoughts will generate positive feelings. What does any of this have to stay young while growing old? —everything! I want to repeat, strength of the mind, starts with what you think and say.

All of us at some point have blamed others what has happened to us, distracting from something good. Turning on negative images must be stopped thinking consciously. Don't get trapped with thoughts that are not rewarding.

Clear your subconscious mind. Tell yourself, that you are starting fresh with a clean slate that past mistakes are just that—past! Today is a new beginning with fresh mental energy. It is wonderful that you have another day to make up for some of the things that you promised yourself you were going to do.

Be thankful that today you have the chance to do a good service for someone, by firstly calling spreading cheer, then doing some errands for them knowing they have been under the weather. A kind gesture works two ways, you feel good the recipient is rewarded. A kindness is the beginning of wisdom.

Years ago, I had a position in a nursing home as their Art Therapist. Coming a few times a week, each person became special, more personal than what my duties called for. I found myself spending extra time feeling sorry when no one came to visit them, writing letters to relatives, and doing errands. I was happy to have had the experience. I felt their love and appreciation in turn, I was the one enriched. But many were old, and the sad part which, I found hard to take was seeing some of them take ill and die.

If you can count two or three things out of your day that you can be grateful for— you my dear are a blessed and happy person.

Recent research shows people who can express gratitude are happier. You've heard me mention the word dopamine. It is a chemical that is released in part of the brain that heightens judgment, and common sense. Studies also show that people who focus on being thankful are able to recover from setbacks quicker. Being aware of gratitude, keeps the stress factor to a minimum in your daily life.

Knowing and focusing on what went right in the day, keeps you in a positive frame of mind. So count your blessings it makes for a balanced life. Balancing your life, requires knowing what is important, what your true priorities are.

Ask yourself simple but important questions—what makes me feel something is missing? What makes me feel satisfied? What do I need to set new priorities so I won't be stressed out, worried?

Taking on new priorities sets your mind to think in a different perceptive. To improve the quality of life "time" seems to be the biggest factor that stands in the way for all. With each moment fast- packed, leaving little time for self and relationships that has you stressed out.

You and you alone have a choice. Remember, that word so often used —choice can help you consciously to decide to build a better life which can bring more time and more satisfaction to your daily work.

Become more aware of where your time goes. How are you spending your time, other than your job? Where are your priorities? If not satisfied, you and you alone, have the power to set your priorities.

CHAPTER 38

Being Mindful

"People are just about as happy as they make up their minds to be."

Abraham Lincoln

Being "mindful" is where we look calmly, objectively at ourselves, and what we do. Living as we do in a busy society, mindfulness forces one to focus on what is taking place in the now, and not things that happened in the past.

It helps us free our thoughts of anxiety. It is important to slow down to take the time to observe what is really going on now, in the present.

I wish I met the man that I read so much about. Bernard Berenson was ninety, a world-famous art historian and humanist. The secret of his happiness was that he knew the art of living. He got sixty minutes from the hour, twenty-four hours from the day.

Berenson added much life to his years by being everlastingly interested in the world around him. Every minute of his time was dedicated, disciplined, and constantly busy, he was never bored, and was full of life - an example for all.

BEING MINDFUL

It is a known fact, that the happiest people are those who have "No time to spare." Mind over matter! What do you want out of your time? How do you spend your moments? Be wise how you put your time to better use.

Remember that word mentioned earlier - selfish. Sing that little tune…tra la! Tra! la! la! Do a little dance—"I'm making time for me, myself, tra la! la! la! la!" Selllllfisssh!

You and those around will find a calmer more relaxed, loving person, and life will be prolonged with less stress. You'll even look better.

With the many things that take up our daily lives, it isn't always easy to understand and act on each emotional feeling that saps our mental energy and resources what we want out of life, and how we achieve it.

The connections between how we think, and our experiences of life control our behavior. All of our past thoughts can be put into our "thought system" how we see the world, every day decisions, reactions, and situations. It is our thought system that enables us to compare new facts or interpretations we have, is motivated by our own thought system.

What our past experiences over our lifetime, how we perceive "the way life is," is filled with our memory of the past. Because of our feelings, they let us know when our thinking is negative and in a bad mood.

Human feelings that are generated from a natural state of mind: being content, love, gratitude—our mind is restful, we see life clearly, we can concentrate, our mind is calm—our mind is not cluttered with thoughts of the past, or judgment how we are doing. Our feelings are like some flashing street lights, letting us know it is necessary to slow down and stop negative thinking getting us to think positive. Only when you have positive feelings about how you see your daily life unfold, hopefully not keeping you in a bad mood, you are able to maintain mental balance and healthy functioning.

Healthy functioning is where you feel wonderful for no particular reason other than your mind is relaxed, free of worry in a positive state of mind. Once you understand that it is you, the power of your mind, that there is little, value being in a funky mood, recognizing moods are connected to feelings.

Human beings are always looking to find happiness. Perhaps too often conditions are attached. Realize that happiness is the ultimate goal and not the means to the goal…I repeat, it is the goal and not the means getting to the goal.

Happiness, once gained, this feeling of happiness is what you have been looking for all along —you reached your goal!

Reflecting on moments that you thought was the ultimate bringing you happiness breeds a happy existence and high spirits and an abundant way of life. It is a positive feeling that exists inside you giving you balance and a feeling of well being.

It was asked of one Buddha, why people tend to experience more unhappiness in their lives than happiness.

He said "part of the answer is quite simple it is because all things are impermanent and ever-changing. Most people carry on their lives and think everything lasts forever."

BEING MINDFUL

Much of the frustration and misery that we experience comes about through a mistaken belief in permanence. We think that our happiness can last forever, and when we lose what we value, we experience unhappiness.

One key to solving problems is to recognize that 'feeling good' is where you want to be, it comes first. Solving the problem comes later. A very important point to understand that problems get worse by the way we feel, rather than by trying to stop circumstances.

When we pay more attention on raising our levels of "feelings," the problems slowly disappear.

Happiness is inherent. It isn't outside your self. It is a natural feeling of your healthy psychological being. When we stop trying to change circumstances and concentrate on raising our "feeling level," our problems slowly fade away. Change alone isn't the key to happiness or solving problems. If you can relate to a time when some kind of approval... award... getting a diploma; after the event what happened, to your happiness? You thought it would last longer.

Thoughts develop with the attention we give them. If we want to solve problems faster stop giving so much thought to the problem in order to see in a fresh way—a new solution.

You would think in the reverse. Think hard about it and it can be easier solved, not so. The mind gets over loaded and confused trying to figure out what to do. By turning away, giving the mind a rest, one can consciously see a new approach.

Life has many, many parts to it. Too often our past memories with its problems and disappointments, cloud our judgment with lingering fear that making a decision hard to reach.

Relax for the moment when the tension builds up, go do something: take in a movie, take a walk, do some exercise. A relaxed state of mind helps you take in more information, and you become less anxious, seeing a way to a new approach to your problems. Having realized some of these things that are ruining your day you can begin to handle what is distracting and getting more mental energy and motivation to help get back on track what your real priorities are.

The saying, "mind over matter," no one knows what is possible to the mind of the human being. Your mind can liberate you from any obstacles, if you let it. You can picture happiness, health and success. Your mental attitude toward the things you picture for yourself, your subconscious mind will help make sure that it happens. What we picture, the power within us can become a reality.

The impact on your attitude on life is more important than circumstance. If you have had financial reversals, personal disappointments do not prolong your despair by reliving these experiences in your mind. Visualize the future with your dreams with its promises that these frustrating moments will pass seeing better what you want in life. See it—it is in your inner mind! The secret is within you. Life is a school. Life is a restless and chaotic stream that we must learn to have the power to ride the waves along to higher and better things.

CHAPTER 39

Find Your Goals

"Acceptance is a sign of courage."

Yanla Vanzant

Persistence takes courage to hold out and be determined to find your goals in spite of the uncertainties you might face. Trying to handle being a mom and a job is hard. There's still a lot of guilt, for there aren't enough hours in the day, trying to be all things to everyone, at the same time understanding that some days you're not at your top of your game as a mom and as an employee. But no one at home will love you less.

There are many new firms that have made a great start in creating a supportive working environment for moms. 96% of top firms offer flexible, schedules and more than a third allow their employees to alter their schedule every week. You might find your voice and offer suggestions to solving stress problems, having on-sight fitness center dealing with tension. Offer yoga classes and stress management counseling. Finding resolutions is all part of what makes your days less stressful knowing that there could be another alternative. Saving a few minutes here and there gives you time for more self.

One hidden advantage of getting older is that your energy level drops a little. This isn't bad for it actually forces you to slow down and pay attention and not rush on to the next thing. Life can become richer sometimes when you slow down, do less and savor more. Having patience with yourself helps you gain peace of mind.

There are too many artificial limits that we set growing older. Your mental fear and inertia, your resistance to change, keeps you from accepting another challenge making life more exciting.

Don't stop - draw on your strength and wisdom. Don't put limits on your potential regardless how old you are. Wisdom is good sense. It is knowledge and experience that you have accumulated over time. You don't stop laughing because you grow old, rather the reverse, you grow old because you stop laughing.

I don't mean to be on a soap box preaching. My message is to show one the big picture using brain power, to help recognize and cope with some of life's hardest to understand problems coming away with less stress living longer.

Besides romantic love, there's love of material possessions. More shopping for more shoes—more stuff! This seeking self gratification never gives one complete contentment.

I have known one gal who goes shopping when down. It makes her feel good. I personally don't think so, because when she gets home, she still hasn't faced what is really bothering her.

Money problems are a number one household conflict, with principles and ideas how to live within a budget, not spending more than one can afford. To reinforce sound attitude that you and only you, have the power how to get the best out of life; using emotional intelligence, reasoning, which helps eliminating stress, staying healthier, happier, slowing down the age process. Whatever results feels comfortable to absorb mentally— call it wisdom for everyday living.

It still boils down to common horse sense, that all can stand hearing to set the mind thinking and learning the art of living each day. It is, understanding more about yourself through each problem that you tackle and over-come with positive benefits.

It would be grand if others we have relationships with see life as we do. Until we know the action and purpose of our partner, knowing ourselves, the issues of our differences will seem less important.

Having too many credit cards is too big a temptation, to keep spending. You can't keep a close enough check on where the money goes. Shifting perspectives, viewing one's, problems from different angles helps.

Getting your financial house in order increases your level of confidence. If you think that you will find the way out of your problem and won't be defeated, your mind is receiving those positive reactions, how you think—it will happen. Staying down doesn't solve your mood.

Be consciously aware that you don't have to have a lot of money to enjoy the loving relationships in the family that help enrich your life. When you learn more about yourself, more honesty, you look to the horizons and make your life better. Stress wears you down. Stress makes you look old, makes you feel, old—it saps your energy.

Nurtured by a flexible mind, you are better able to adapt to new situations, and allows one to fully embrace all of life. But thinking logically and creatively being accountable and not staying in a state of worry over financial problems takes more than you, but family cooperation to help put their heads together and solve the problem.

That makes me wonder how much is your family involved each other and their interests—each as a family supporting the other. Just listening to problems, even if trivial, is important to another. Concern showing love that each of us so badly crave and so often we're so busy, we forget to show each other gratitude, appreciation for family—the fabric of our lives.

When you think of dysfunctional families that bring nothing to the table, excuse my metaphor of speech—none are in harmony. There is too much inertia— disinterest. It takes thinking attitude, nurturing, honesty, responsibility, appreciation, respect, to make a family work.

One parent or both set the examples. It has to be and can be, regardless of how financially fit the family is. One thing has nothing to do with the other.

As a concerned family, it gives one the opportunity for airing out experiences, thinking, molding strength of character, respect to work in harmony, honesty; being able to openly discuss having differences of opinions in the midst of all the heated shouts, without feeling intense aggression or anger.

Some of my family are Democrats some Republicans. We have had some heated discussions, getting together at this time of the year, when in not too many months away, there will be another election for the President of the United States. Thank goodness we all hugged and felt if nothing more, we had a brain work out, which left us stimulated, thinking.

Life at times becomes over powering. There are good reasons to lament negative feelings, sometimes to a friend, just don't over due it. Friends are great to pour out your troubles, but it can cause a rift when the friend is over burdened. Understandably they're not too eager to be with you, they have their own problems.

Worry! Depression! Tension! Fears! An emotional state of mind that plays havoc on your health, draining you from feeling young while growing old.

Talking feelings out helps us recognize and think differently and can help to let go and move on with new spirit and hope. Hope is a powerful thought. It is the light in a dark tunnel.

Most of us do not keep an eye on our thoughts, mind over matter and so most of the time have no idea what we are clearly thinking. Doubting that we won't achieve what we want at the out come only makes matters worse, filling us with fear and tension raising our blood pressure, jeopardizing our health. Let's not forget…stress makes us grow old before our time. Think before you fall under your mental spell of non- rationalization. If you think about your past problems you realize that you came to a conclusion, using reasonable facts of evidence and didn't dwell upon what went wrong, but concentrated on working upon correcting the outcome. That's having rational, positive thinking. Read this paragraph over again.

Many times we pull back from doing what we want to do because of fear. Fear comes in many different forms. It takes overcoming feeling unworthy. The more what you know about your abilities to cope with uncertainties, you can master your fears, which helps give strength to your convictions. We contribute in general to our emotional distress replaying again in our mind the painful memories, which many a times, are self- created. It is reinforcing negative emotions making matters worse. Over reacting to things of less importance, how you respond with reasoning to a given situation is what keeps you balanced.

Unhappiness comes to each of us because, we think ourselves at the center of the world, because we have a conviction that we alone suffer to the point of unbearable incidents. Unhappiness is always to feel oneself confined in one's own skin, in one's own brain—"it can only happen to me! I don't deserve this!" Scientists start with the premise that all of our thoughts are functions of chemical reaction to the brain. There are many factors at play for achieving lasting happiness though difficult, it is possible.

CHAPTER 40

Keep Optimistic

"Does it ever occur to you that you can't lose anything because you never had it in the first place? The only thing you've ever really had is yourself."

Deepak Chopra

If you are not troubled with mental illness then you are capable of controlling your mental attitude setting forth basic behavior, with proper direction.

Having conscious control of your subconscious mind; to draw upon your creative powers what things in life you desire, and the determination to work to achieve it. Maintaining an optimistic state of mind and the power of right thinking, are some basic reminders to hang on to, in fulfilling your life, you will answer to —"I am a happy person!"

Do you remember Christopher Reeve, the actor who was thrown from a horse and suffered a spinal cord injury that left him paralyzed from the neck down? On being interviewed, he was asked how he was coping. It was natural to be depressed, once so active, now helpless.

KEEP OPTIMISTIC

As the weeks and months went by he realized how fortunate he didn't have brain injury and had plans to speak and educate the public about his spinal cord injury to help others. He felt blessed having a loving devoted wife and children who gave him the strength to continue to promote further work on spinal cord injuries and actually considered himself to be a 'lucky guy!'

He was a prime example of maintaining an optimistic state of being. He drew upon the creative powers of his mind. His courage was inspiring and thankful that he had a mind, which helped him stay alive and yes feel like—"a lucky guy!" He found something positive to hold onto in spite of his being severally handicapped, which altered his life. Using some simple, but hard thought patterns it carried him along daily to think in a positive, creative way—to help others in similar situations and to enlighten the public about those with spinal cord injury. He was grateful that there were advances being further studied, finding a cure, hopefully in his life time.

How many of us under unfortunate conditions could have maintained his wonderful attitude? He didn't dwell on his disability, but was projecting and making plans, keeping his mind positive. He never lived long enough to carry out some of his wishes. But his wife has taken up the challenge, making sure that continued medical research on spinal cord will go forth.

Human beings are thinking creatures. The more we understand the process and force of thought to be the foundation to living we can have a fully functional and happy life.

STAY YOUNG TO 100

As Deepak Chopra said, wise thought gives insight on the truth involving all of us, after everything is said and done, the only thing we ever have is self. Knowing who we are, understanding more about self as we mature; how we live out our life with compassion for others. We should be rewarded with contentment. With very little exception, we humans who are exposed to understanding the process of thought are able to use common-sense solutions to every day problems.

Common sense is sound practical judgment based on reason. What we all want is that positive feeling state in ourselves, which comes about by not concentrating on our problems, which more often only makes things worse. Stepping aside and diverting your thoughts, you will come to a solution quicker. How is your judgment, your common sense?

It is all important showing one's maturity. You have learned as we discussed more about your thoughts. That thinking is a wonderful gift, providing you have the ability to think positive enriching your life.

Is seems simple, "all you have to do is think positive." but the longer we live, the more we add to our memory bank holding onto the past with all the blunders and regrets.

The truth is, it is easy to change your thinking providing you don't let life get in the way. It takes creating a life and concentrating on what you really want. Most of us have certain times when we are clearheaded and our energy level is high. Decision making then comes easy.

It is difficult to satisfy our mind not to stray when we lack passion for what we are doing. To focus is sometimes hard. It is not inherent. Often times we find concentrating difficult on assignments we don't like. When this is the case, ask yourself, what part of this do I care about? It makes you focus better. Train yourself not to be distracted by removing anything that is not relevant to what you're doing. Music should be quiet and soothing.

Remember to focus on what is important. If the assignment is too overwhelming, your mind will turn off to keep from being overburdened. Drinking caffeine can stimulate but it lasts the most 60 minutes.

Your new job can sometimes make you anxious. More than one-third of Americans report having had a panic attack. A panic attack is where an anxiety alarm to the body responds and kicks in even though there is no life-threatening danger. Low blood sugar can copy a panic attack. It doesn't hurt to see a doctor if it happens more than once when you feel anxiety.

You can learn to manage your anxiety. For example: during an attack don't think the worse "I'm having a heart attack!" Calm your thoughts and let yourself know that you are just anxious. Your good reasoning will help.

Your emotional well-being is learning to control, and cope with life's problems. When you better understand self and others; you will be able to handle making better decisions, and find that your life is happier and purposeful.

Once a week set aside take fifteen minutes and sit away somewhere not disturbed, and think calmly how your week went. Where you very happy? Moderately happy? Down? Do you know why you had these feelings? Think - Work through your thoughts, don't deny truths. Were children involved? Spouse? The job? How much did you contribute to the problem? Questions!

One wonders why bad things happen to good people so much of the time. Is it that they are not aware that opportunity is staring them in the face, because of doubts, fears stop short, having the will to take hold and pursue their ultimate goal?

Having conscious control of your subconscious mind is what gives you a map to lay out the path, to picture mentally the things you desire for the now and the future. Not completing something you started because you lost interest isn't the best constructive way to deal with anything in life.

I had a very good teacher, my husband, who never started anything that he didn't finish. He once remarked about a book he was reading, how he found it uninteresting. I remarked, in a flippant manner, "Well, why read it?" His reply, "it's a bad habit to get into, which carries over into more important things in life." It brought to my attention about something that just had happened to me.

Living on our ranch, while removing the wash off the clothes line, as I started to step into the house, glancing back over my shoulder, I saw one small child's pants flapping in the breeze. For a brief moment, I stared at it and wondered why I left it when, I surely could have included it along with the other things in the basket. I went back and retrieved it and began to think hard.

The more I thought of this small incident, it occurred to me that I had done similar things before; there was a pattern that I became use too, never bothering to follow through, never going that extra mile to conclusion. That day was the turning point. Just this simple act caused me to become aware and helped me change my attitude and turn-about my actions. I never start something now that I don't finish.

Reflecting on my childhood, I never was asked to do many things, for most things were done for me. When I did undertake something, if disinterested, I walked away with no parent telling me to stay with it. I analyzed what my thinking was about. Doubt that the finished product would not be good enough…fear…lack of confidence? Probably was all part of me plus—I wasn't taught discipline.

Being married to Sam helped give me the courage to carry out my vision of what, I wanted to do and be. On his shoulders, I flew. Having conscious control over my subconscious mind was the beginning, understanding the reverse of my negative mental images. Now older, wiser the knowledge learned over the years have, helped me understand in general what life is about. Firstly it was learning who I was. That first step opened channels in my behavior for the better.

In stressful moments, I was better able to stay calm and listen to my inner-voice guiding me knowing I had better smarts to handle a bad situation. What we take from, each day determines how well–being we will be. What we take away unconsciously, from our parents determines how certain things we react to during our life time. How we think has to do with our strength or lack of mental maturity.

Many unsolved bad situations come about by one's lack of emotional maturity. It is sometimes good to question about your emotional maturity. Do you have reasonable self-confidence to see you through handling adversities? Do you have a hold on reality so that what makes sense in terms of cause and effect? Adding it up, a healthy, mature person has good human relationships. How do you rate?

Learning who we are is an important step, it makes us think and question the "whys" for our actions and what we plan to do about it. It takes being responsible for our own lives. Too often the same mistakes are made over and over so one has to think about judgment.

It is hard knowing if our decisions are always correct. If you have a bad attitude that life did you wrong, you are not being responsible. If you blame others for making you do things you do not wish —you're not responsible—no one can make you think and do something as a grown person that you don't want too, unless they have a choke hold on you.

So when you stop and think, how have you been handling situations? Have you taken responsibility to make a wrong— right? It means being accountable. That's a very good word to hang your actions on. Your change of attitude, facing up to who you are and realizing what you want out of your days is being accountable—responsible?

Are you consciously aware what things are bringing you down? Confront your subconscious mind. Listen to your inner-voice. Question your attitude, is it healthy? Knowing the rewards can be positive what will you do to be more accountable, live effectively feel happier, a sense of well being? These are some of the emotional rewards.

Acquiring a positive state of mind isn't a quick fix. It takes mind over matter, staying calm, thinking it all out. It takes courage, determination, honesty to dig deep inside and help find answers. Get, your power of thoughts in order.

Mental control is the secret of "mature judgment." That's what you strive for when you reach the proper age when the law says you can drive, and you come of age to go to a bar and have a drink.

Mature judgment is what and how decisions are made. It's wisdom, it's good sense.

CHAPTER 41

Correcting a Negative Image

"There is no such thing in anyone's life as an unimportant day."

Alexander Woollcott

There's more than one approach to correcting a negative picture, choice comes into play. Some people can never make even one decision. Spend more time and energy on a decision, only if something will give you significantly better results is how to act upon.

The notion of "it will do!" Feels like you're settling for second best thing. But settling still is good, it's better than nothing. Whether how significantly short-term the impact will affect your life, spend less time making the decision.

When a decision is final you go through a variety of strong psychological processes that please you knowing your decision, or choice was as good considering the alternative. Decisions can be over something trivial at the moment or more serious. Looking back whether you made the right choice at something you should have done is foolish thinking.

CORRECTING A NEGATIVE IMAGE

Once I had lunch with a friend, who remarked on seeing an old boyfriend. She laughingly said that he still looked surprisingly great. As an afterthought, my friend started making comparisons reflecting whether, she could have done better.

I thought she was better off thinking, what her choice made twelve years ago. Unless terribly unhappy, foolishly she would make herself miserable thinking, "I could have done better!" Leave it alone!

Temptation is always around. There is the possibility to see better-looking, more prosperous than what you have. I was relieved and pleased hearing her say, "my choice was made a long time ago when, I recognized qualities that matched me perfectly!"

One rule you should not be hasty or choosing blindly making any decision. The important serious ones, give yourself a certain amount of time to review, and a time to make a choice.

On a lighter vein, if it comes to making a purchase, it isn't necessary to always research products after you make a decision. If your, so incline, do this before hand than you will feel sure and safe. Perhaps you know someone like my cousin, who finds it always difficult making even a small decision. It was exhausting hearing when shopping for a new sofa, found something she liked, after walking her feet off in more stores than you could count.

She still had to go to "just one more!" And still wasn't completely one hundred percent sure, what she bought was right. Asking me over and over and others, what did they think. With so little confidence having this mind set, one doesn't feel they did the right thing and there would be consequences. Judgment is a process of mind, the ability to think in a logical manner that helps you make sound decisions.

One quality which many times hinders the judgment is uncontrolled emotional reaction to people and situation. How do you get to judgment— to choice? Your great tool is your mind. With, your mind gives you courage, power over all conditions.

Our success, our future, our happiness, is our strong mind. That part of the mind, which helps to remember, have understanding and think, too often we aren't making good use of our mind. Learn that your time is important. Don't misuse it by trying to make a perfect choice.

Who's perfect? Is it necessary to be? If the goal is always to attain perfection, it is too much to ask of oneself, and harder for those around. Perhaps, if working at something that calls for precision, as an example in the science world, where accurate application is required. Then being thorough— a stickler type, would make this person right for the job.

When a demanding job takes up all your time and energy, this is the moment to remember that you have to be in charge of your life. Without a strong foundation knowing how to delegate and hand over tasks, one cheats one's self of simple pleasures, the joys of life.

Eliminate what saps your energy. Find someone who will do your errands, those small things that free your time. With new priorities you can begin to take control of what is really important and your true desires.

The way you think, and how you spend your time, choice is what moves you ahead. Knowing that you have alternatives that can change your life, that can make a difference. Knowing your priorities over time will change. Conditions make it so.

Stop and ask yourself:

Have you used your time wisely?

Have you been remiss on what's important in this time of your life? Have you put off too long making your dreams a reality?

With the hustle and bustle of our sandwich pack full lives, it is very important to pause, and —get off the merry- go- round. One owes it to themselves what their priorities are by shifting one's perspective making new comparisons, finding new positive ways to lessen the stress on the body and mind, which can take just so much before it breaks down health wise…making you look old.

The idea of doing something as simple as having a schedule at work when you take a twenty minute break, and putting a note on your door with the time you will be back, letting whoever you work with know that you need a few minutes to catch-up. Relax, putting everything aside, stay put make sure no calls will disturb you. Kick off your shoes, close your eyes, do some easy meditation breathe deeply block everything from your mind.

The other alternative will be to leave the office and start walking briskly for twenty minutes, if time permits make it longer. This will relieve your over stimulated mind and relieve the tension building up in your system. You'll be back energized able to put your refreshed mind to better use. The toll on women executives in high positions has passed men in having stress related breakdowns.

The ever present pressure in big business to retain their leadership is having companies be clever at casting dissatisfaction in consumers, to get them to buy more expensive products, when something less is more than adequate.

For you the consumer, today with so many companies fighting for your business, don't hesitate to speak to the manager and ask if he couldn't do better on the price. Go to the top first, the salesperson has little clout.

Every business person can relate to a story about a highly skilled executive who was promoted into a high leadership position only to fail on the job. Another person, with intellectual abilities and technical skills who was promoted into a similar position —climbed to the top. How come?

Emotional intelligence: is to be able to work with others. The importance thinking and seeing the big picture having foresight with emotional intelligence is critical affecting the job.

Emotional intelligence: is vital to solutions that one had more then the other. Without it, a person can have the best training, a lot of smart ideas he or she brings to the table— it isn't enough. What is needed is emotional intelligence.

Emotional intelligence: is brainpower. It is having mental control, good creative judgment which gives one, logical thinking.

Emotional intelligence: is having wisdom over things that can defeat you.

When we read about Christopher Reeve, he possessed that important quality of mental control, Emotional intelligence, which helped him think courageously and made his days livable.

Natural impulses drive our emotions. If you go only on emotion, you are not clear thinking and your mind is not suitable for making sound judgment. Keeping mental control you will have good judgment not to do worrisome things alone. Don't hesitate to ask for help.

People who become ill with a disease, not able to work, with little or no health insurance, the best thing is to find a support group as, family and friends people who care about you. They will be there to help you make decisions, and help keep you balanced so that you don't run frantic and keep your anxiety level to a minimum.

Today is Veterans Day. I called my son who lives in California to see how he's doing. As a young man of nineteen, he enlisted to fight in the Viet Nam war. His dad and I couldn't talk him out of it…"it's my patriotic duty!" He was fortunate to only have suffered minor physical injuries. His emotional injuries took much longer to heal. Seeing so much action, what he experienced he was lucky, he came out of it alive.

CHAPTER 42

Anger and Hurts

"I shall never stoop so low as to hate any man."

Booker T. Washington

I was surprised hearing my son relate a story just home from the war. One evening going to a party, he was confronted with a hostile remark. "Murderer! How many children did you kill?" He never answered and left with those shouts ringing in his ears. My son had a strong commitment to his country. It really hurt hearing those comments. He almost laid down his life for his country.

Human beings who aren't pleased with life, in return find fault, with everything around them. They're difficult to be near, they go through life with closed minds, which make their world, narrow. They are grouchy, unhappy and they experience limited days feeling happiness.

People who act out, wanting to strike out on others, make themselves feel important. They get an emotional charge with their anger and unfair treatment to others.

They trust no one and have little patience, which, shows a lack of understanding and growth. They listen without much value or respecting ideas, beliefs, opinions that others can have individual differences. There can be a multitude of reasons for a disagreeable personality. I came to my own conclusion why this type person is so mean spirited. It could be having a low opinion of self.

We could reflect on one's childhood environment, rarely if ever being reinforced, positive— lack, of love, lack of attention. A damaged self image carried over into adulthood finds drugs as an outlet, escaping ones own torment. Sometimes it takes only one to intervene to get the person back positive, an asset to society.

Many American men suffer from under diagnosed condition known as Irritable Male Syndrome. It is coined by a Scottish researcher, Dr. Gerald Lincoln.

He found that when the testosterone levels in the animals that he was doing some research on, when the testosterone levels dropped, they became more irritable, sometimes the reversed, being lethargic and moody. One moment he might be impatient, angry, annoyed, touchy, stressed. These people are very hard to live with, snapping at you and the people they work with.

There are reasons for a bad attitude, but going through life with a chip on one's shoulder, no one has the time to try, or want to understand the bad attitude. It takes one to do some soul searching and want to change.

Men who view the world through, "irritable lenses." act out everything negative. A good way to help keep it all in check is regular hard exercise, which increases brain levels of serotonin.

One has to question why, some people can shake off unforeseen bad incidents while others use the misfortunate as excuses, to evoke pity, trying to play on the sympathy of others.

Our conscious mind makes us aware, we are thinking wrong things—we don't feel good. If we are not able to find a solution to our problems, we are thinking in a non-rationale way. Under these conditions, the outcome proves negative.

Thought can be harmful or logical only you can change your thought pattern. Only you can make your life easier when you learn to listen to your inner self with positive feelings, of your inherent mental purpose. The sensible, logical, reasonable thing is change. Stop how you have been thinking and start rethinking new thoughts which will be rewarding feelings, coming from your positive attitude.

When you understand that concentrating on the negative, believing that the problem is hopeless, only reinforces your negative attitude and the mind listening, follows an unreasonable conclusion.

The outlook is gloomy keeping one in a low mood. Thoughts set your mood. Mood is part of life. We all experience highs and lows. Taking our mind off whatever it is on, the mood should pass. Thoughts in a low mood will be distorted and because our feelings are the results of what we think, so will our feelings be distorted. You look through life through your thought process, not with your normal state of mind.

Thinking is closely connected with the activity of certain specific nerve cells in the brain. No one knows for sure how the nerve cells work when you are thinking. Scientists believe we have ten or twelve billion nerve cells.

ANGER AND HURTS

It is questionable that we remember things the way they are. We remember them the way we think they should have been. We work on our memories until they fit patterns we already have in our minds. It is hardly ever exact and all very complicated.

We don't see just with our eyes, we also see with our brain. What you see almost depends as much on you, on your life's experience and much more.

Perception is a key to your personality. To your awareness, how you observe things. How keen is your insight— it's your opinion. Some of us have great intuition, giving a sixth sense to an incident.

We speak about this as one being clairvoyant— intuitive, the ability being psychic can see beyond this life. My oldest sister had a touch of it. She would tell me, giving me reasons that I'd best listen to her. Her insight speaking about perception on situations was very keen.

Age and wisdom sometimes go together. That gives one a certain amount of clairvoyance. From time to time perhaps you too felt that you had some mystic powers. It all ties into the brain with reflection and thought.

If thinking in the same unproductive way, it will not change what we do to alter our mood. Whenever we are feeling angry, unhappy, depressed, these feelings are our own thought system.

These emotions can destroy personal relationships. Besides it destroys one's health. Hostility has harmful effects and is a major effect in heart disease, high cholesterol and high blood pressure, and of course aging if you still live your life out to a normal age.

How to overcome acting out anger? One has to work on patience and tolerance. It takes making a concerted effort to control feelings. The realization of your mind spinning into hateful thoughts are thoughts generated from one holding on to emotional state of anger and hurts, not necessarily what is taking place at the present incident, but on something done to them from the past. Certain strong emotions harboring anger and hate must be checked before hand.

What is in the subconscious mind must be reasoned with, and brought forth to the conscious mind to continue to talk to, when starting to lose control and become hostile. Having patients and tolerance, proves acting with thought and reasonable emotion letting go of anger and getting a different perspective, looking from a different angle—more to forgive than hate.

Again do not regress into the past of what has happened, but think with a cool brain with tolerance and have the strength to walk away then stay and shout words of hate and resentment trying to get the last word.

With it all, what did you gain? Who came out the winner? Fighting for position only caused damage to your entire system. Hateful words caused lingering resentment to the other person in your life.

As the younger generation so aptly put it—"cool it!" I've been saying in somewhat different ways, throughout the many chapters of this book. The secret lies within us—in you! To achieve happiness learn more about self. In so doing, you will understand more about others.

We don't live on an island alone. With people that we relate too, with every action, there's a reaction. The more we get to know another person, the more open we become. When there is greater understanding, there is an awareness a sensitivity, a mindfulness of the other person's feelings and point of view. Many issues will become less.

No two people see everything the same because of the individual life's experience. We all come together bringing our emotional baggage, which if we can work through makes for greater understanding, a harmonies relationship, gaining greater respect.

Feeling insecure brings about someone's bad attitude. Getting to the root of these feelings might be not receiving enough attention. Man is a nurturing being, who needs love. That could be another reason.

An important thought, strike the word "I" from your vocabulary think, "You." When you have positive things to share you'll find that you are less overwhelmed by your problems and interested in the other person.

CHAPTER 43

It Is Up To You

"Measure not life by enjoyment but rather what you shall be, than backward to what you have been."

Anonymous

Every day should be important. "But it is all up to you!" You are the only person who can use their ability to get you where you want to be, never losing sight, being persistent, continuing steadily, despite obstacles.

Does that sound easier said than can be? Not at all! With good thinking some obstacles that are hindering require pushing fear aside, using rational solutions to a new approach

Sometimes we contribute to our own unhappiness, exaggerating something out of proportion. Without being aware, we contribute to making a situation worse by fanning the fire with angry words better left well enough alone.

Thinking is hard. Thinking requires honesty, to face the reality to confront the problems. Trying to find positive solution takes thinking. Because thinking is hard, we put off. Apathy sets in. Problems are difficult to solve. We want solutions to come easy. Figuring how requires clear, hard thinking.

It takes logic, reasoning, common sense, which helps with a strong mind to be better able to solve the many complex problems confronted with. Following a different direction sometimes and sort out positive behavior many of the problems become less.

The obstacles that stand in our way for reaching our goals and happiness is that we have the knowledge to make our lives good, but like a broken record we keep playing out our past problems not learning to be wise from the experience, to sound reasoning changing positive patterns.

By changing your focus opens you to new solutions. If you were advising a friend how would you suggest getting over this? Look for and point out what others are doing right. It's great for your mental strength to be able to share positive things.

Contributing makes our own problems that much less important. We aren't alone if we share and try and help someone.

"Logic" is the system of reasoning. The philosophy theory of reasoning deals with distinguishing good from bad. Have you ever met someone who is intelligent but has poor reasoning faculties, which keeps them from making wise choices? We blame it on lack of maturity.

Thinking a way of life is most helpful. There will always be trouble. It is our attitude that will help us gain control over it.

Emotional Intelligence, is having brain power. For some people a lack of it hampers them from making proper decisions. Being in touch with your gut instinct or your inner wise-self will keep you moving in the right positive path.

Have you ever had a gut feeling about something which was not in your best interest? Sometimes one should listen to some basic inner feelings to help make sound choices.

Intuition is knowing instinctively that something isn't right. You become suspicious, which can save you from some dangerous incident. Very young children have not learned this and are prone to misjudging where to go and with whom. The longer we live, with our life's experience we should become wiser.

The more humans became civilized the more there instinctive unconscious qualities diminished which is basic knowing automatically. We think we don't need it, but it safe guards us incase of danger.

When I lived in Chicago, in high school, my girlfriend wanted to meet our other friend who lived on the other side of Garfield Park. It was growing dark and threatening, I wanted her not to walk but to take the bus. She didn't want to wait shouting back, "the exercise will do me good!"

I didn't like the idea her walking alone in the park at this time. I had a bad feeling. She laughed at me and said I was a worrier. As she walked off, I remember calling out, "be careful!"

It was late evening when her boyfriend called, and said Betty never returned home, he was very worried. As it was he had cause to be, she was attacked and brutally beaten and left for dead.

IT IS UP TO YOU

When I visited Betty in the hospital, I was shocked seeing her bruised face. It was painful to witness what she looked like. Reassured my first strong instincts— common reasoning at the time told me her actions weren't sound. She was fortunate that she lived.

Bravery is one thing in its place, but what she did walking without caution was fool hardy. These are actions of a child being reckless.

Encountering a mishap can teach one a bitter lesson that can last a life time. It defeats the purpose, making daily life stressful full of fears and tension to overcome. It is difficult overcoming a bad happening. Your thoughts can take you from calm one moment into a state of panic, relieving those horrific moments.

I know that Betty never walked alone at night again in the park. It was a long road to recovery for my friend, who had flashbacks reliving that night.

Focusing on something in the present that is pleasant gets you slowly relaxed. Feeling less stressed brings one back in the moment. In charge taking command of positive thoughts, you drive fear from your consciousness and your life forever. Life's experiences make you face reality.

Happiness is a feeling. When you concentrate on your feelings being happy, your mind is calm, you are thinking with positive, common sense. Staying with the proper attitude, shifting thoughts, finding another angle to think upon under very trying time period, greater understanding is achieved then to negative feelings.

Only you have the capacity to choose what you think about. If you choose to think about past hurts, you will continue to feel bad.

STAY YOUNG TO 100

While it is very true you can't change the effect past influences had on you once, you can change the effect they have on you now.

Stay Young, at least to 100 one thing for sure, keeping your mind sharp in shape. Keeping on top of events. Keeping in the present moment. Make every minute count. Don't take life for granted that you will remain healthy and ward off Alzheimer's.

Research shows that brain health is closely linked to the health of our hearts and blood vessels. In the same way that muscles and bones benefit from strength training in the gym. Our brains benefit from mental activity. The key is to select activities that are different and complex.

Things that are a challenge to your mind are very important and stimulating. Learn a language, take up playing an instrument. Think about taking in an interesting lecture.

I went the other week with friends to the Hall of Science in Chicago. An hour and a half drive to see and hear the lecture of Charles Darwin's theory of Evolution. I was delighted that they had insisted that I join them. I had been in a rut, working too much by myself. My brain was over worked, over tired.

One doesn't have to believe in Darwin's theory, but to learn more about the man was very interesting. It opened channels in my brain, giving thought I never considered thinking about.

The change, and being with friends, driving back home afterwards comparing impressions about the event was stimulating. It carried over the following day refreshed and my energy level high. Different moments like this is what we all need from time to time. It keeps us feeling energized. Change even for a few hours, gives the brain a chance to view the day differently in a more relaxed mode.

"One of the secrets of a happy life is continuous small treats."

Iris Murdoch

It's a known fact that families don't read anymore and exchange ideas with stimulating thoughts. Television is fine, computers are fine, but spending hours in front of them excludes anyone else in your life. No one is exchanging enough face to face thoughts. Kids go from school to their computers and sit for hours till supper. Families that eat dinner together lower their stress. Studies have been made that there is less juvenile delinquency. If one has a family there must be an exerted effort, to change the life style or patterns if we want to see the children grow mature and healthy.

Your great tool is your mind. Mind gives control. Our successes, our happiness, our future, are all determined in the mind. The ability to think is the real essence of human beings.

CHAPTER 44

Challenge Yourself

"A man without a purpose is like a ship without a rudder."

Carlyle

Challenge yourself, it will keep you on your toes. Energies alter your down mood to a happy high spirit. People who constantly keep repeating, "I'm bored!" They are without a question—boring! People who are bored with life are not living life. They are not using their minds for best results, getting the most out of life.

Put some meaning into your life; sometimes just reorganizing your daily schedule, you get a new charge of energy. You can't be bored if active and interested in everything. The more you are involved with things the more you stay healthy. Getting with a new mix of interesting people with alive-minds eager to do interesting things, keeps you mentally alive and keeps you perpetually staying young growing old.

As I have referred before, "the mind is you!" The brain is where we understand, think and remember. That is the essence of you.

CHALLENGE YOURSELF

If quiet is what you seek, get away from the noise relax, find peace and quiet with a book. If not far from a park with a lagoon rent a boat, it is mentally invigorating and relaxing. Anything different from what you do daily knocks boredom out. Learn to play a sport, knock some balls around. Find something that gets you out of the house— get off your duff!

Friends are very important. Friends that are thinkers are good. Don't spend time with people who are lamenting "life is boring!" You don't need that.

Psychological stress - the more nerve racking it becomes the more what you are doing needs analyzing. If that tiresome job is mind-numbing, tedious than slowly look for another. Keep at it, and you'll find something better. Change is never easy, but it can be the best thing ever. What stands in the way of most discussion is fear. I can't help mentioning again that word, "Fear." It holds one back from wanting change badly enough. Think of all the moments that you wanted to venture out making a change that would really make a difference in your life. But fear held you back. What makes you hesitate applying for it, the uncertainly—fear!

Much of our fear has to do with self-acceptance. Forget about mistakes, they happen to all. Live with the thought that you are a valuable worthwhile human being, because you exist.

You are one of a kind. There is no one like you. Your finger print is one of a kind. There are so many reasons that make you special, indispensable, simply because you exist. You make a difference! Have patience with all things, but first with being who you are. Never forget never confuse your value as a human being. At times we all face self-doubt, but that should only be temporary, not a permanent character flaw. Like yourself! It helps to like others.

I've misplaced who said the quote or where it came from, but it is something to think about. "If you think you're too small to make a difference, you haven't been in bed with a mosquito."

That should leave you with self-acceptance for we sometimes are our worse critic. Finding fault with self is a natural bad habit we all have and must look for the positive sides.

People who live alone over a long period of time, who made this choice have a tendency to grow old sooner. Humans do better, in a nurturing environment. They stay healthier and look better. To give one's love and receive is as important as good nutrients that boost libido.

Perhaps a disappointing relationship has discouraged you and turned you away from again sharing a life. To live with fear which many do, the cause and affect so hurtful; left with fearing if they do such and such this will happen again, so they never do it.

No one should go through life alone. It is better you share your life with someone. Our basic human instincts is to love and care for each other. We do better and live longer if we are with someone. I've said it before, we are nurturing beings. Relationships aren't always easy, but a life alone isn't easy either.

It is the belief of some people that it is better to let small bothersome things go by, and only be concerned with big issues. Actually it's the little things that add up and wear down relationships.

There are times in our lives when we know we need a change, but are held back by fear. The feeling of being stuck increases our sense of powerlessness. We have a lot of anger.

Sherry Lansing, a former movie executive always loved the movies. She wanted to make movies was laughed at, but that didn't discourage her. The day she graduated from College with a degree to teach English and math, she packed her bags and headed out to Los Angles and got a job paying $5 dollars an hour reading scripts and worked her way up. She worked her way to running Fox Studios. There she met her husband, a big director.

She had power and success but after many successful movies to her credits such as—"Fatal Attraction" and "The Accused." She woke one morning feeling restless and wanted a change. No time for personal life, she was putting in 900 hours a day and felt she didn't have the quality of life that she wanted. She loved her old life and new life, but time moved on, Sherry Lansing wanted her life to have some social relevance to it.

Her world expanded, She started a movement called Prime Time, which takes people who are retired so that they can give back. She formed teaching programs where retirees go back to school to get their teaching credentials.

A person who wanted a change, something new, she took the bull by the horns wasn't afraid to make a change, and today is very gratified with her new life style.

Again always trying to make her life meaningful more fulfilling, worked hard and started another foundation, which is dedicated to cancer research and to health. "Every day is filled with something new," Sherry says. She is a women complete.

Live in the moment. Live in the here and now. Listen to your inner-voice. Too often we put off what we always wanted— that is lazy thinking. Putting off for some other time, when you retire in five years? In five years you might not be around! Live for the moment! Perhaps that trip to Spain? If it isn't money then what is stopping you?

Make time it will give you passion, and energy that you need to deal with some of the frustrations of day-to-day living. It could be being in a rut, and letting the years creep up, without feeling you accomplished anything nearer, what you long dreamed about having.

Be courageous, you only have one body, one life. Go out on a limb and get some of the sweet fruit. Life has much to offer. "It," is such an important pronoun—a point of view.

My point of view— nothing ventured, nothing gained. Take time other than the Christmas season to remember to do something nice for your fellow-humans. Giving and receiving pleasure has its reward.

CHAPTER 45

Everyone Needs a Smile

"One cannot think well, love well, if one doesn't use their mind well."

Anonymous

The other day as I entered the bus, glancing about for a seat, I was suddenly aware how the people looked drained, so worn out. Their expressionless face revealed much to me. It was a quick observation, but the overall impression was so powerful that, I wanted to reach out and say something cheerful.

I started to smile at the lady seated next to me. She slowly smiled back and it opened up a dialogue. I made a comment, what a lovely spring day it was with the flowers beginning to bloom. With the idle chatter, I asked if she had a garden. Her reply was "no, she wished she did, she lived in an apartment." I mentioned did she ever think of a small herb garden on her kitchen window sill? Her eyes lit up, "no, she never thought of this." As she stood to leave, she thanked me, her smile was so nice. I turned and smiled at two elderly women seated across from me—they slowly smiled back.

EVERYONE NEEDS A SMILE

That evening I had to make a speech at a Kiwanis Club. I thought hard, what should it be? With the problems of the times, I settled on:

"Everyone needs a smile."

Smiling is infectious, you catch it like the flu, when someone smiled at me today, I started smiling too, I passed around the corner and someone saw my grin, when he smiled, I realized I'd passed it on to him. I thought about that smile, then realized its worth, a single smile just like mine, could travel round the earth.

So if you feel a smile begin, don't leave it undetected, remember, one small smile, mends broken hearts, lifts broken spirits, turns about broken dreams, leaving only positive thoughts for tomorrow.

By the end of the meeting and the social afterwards with everyone smiling and commenting how they enjoyed the talk, there wasn't a sore face around.

In a wonderful illustrated book..."Orestes the Art of Smiling" by Domenico Gnoli, he mentions in one of the chapters about defining the smile by the weight of the nose on the mouth.

The fact that the shape of the smile is the result of an unequal distribution of weight along the line of the lips. Different noses therefore, produce different smiles.

There's many types of smiles: there's a loving smile, a sarcastic smile, the mysterious smile, truly Machiavellian smile, that hides both 'yes' and 'no.' Of course this was only some silly theory. Did it bring a smile to your face? I hope so.

None of us smile enough. An open smile warms the heart when a smile is returned— I like to smile. It is much better than frowning. With many experiencing sadness these days with the war on, the loss of a loved one, every small gesture goes a long way with our emotional psyche.

We are nurturing beings and live longer if we reach out and help someone with nothing more than a hug, and a smile to carry us through the hard days. Being aware how your mind functions allows you right of entry to happiness—a grand feeling which enables you to be welcome and enjoyed by your relationship with family and friends.

The thing about that wonderful feeling contentment, it isn't permanent. So you have to strive a little harder to deal with each problem. Common sense should help you to see alternatives. Once you understand psychologically how we function and our companion, we gain more respect how better to hold on to happiness, for each of us. Happiness is contentment, pleasure, cheerfulness.

The word happiness brings all these thoughts to one's mind. You want that! The key to it is using your mind with wisdom and common sense. Understanding relationships are hard sometimes. If we are basically content than we can deal with more understanding of others. We are less critical, less stressed, more open minded. Judgment is passed without hearing the other one out.

Psychologically everyone functions in the same way. Human beings all have a thought system. We have bad moods—feelings is two way —yours and theirs. By paying attention to your feelings, they get you closer to helping understand your highs and low moods— less stressed.

EVERYONE NEEDS A SMILE

On the flip side of contentment, and happiness, is the contrast that life is filled with suffering, which all of us are touched by and it tests our strength of mind.

The Jewish people have their Talmud, a book of Jewish law that says, "Everything God does, He does for the best."

Buddhist and Hindu believe suffering is a result of our own negative past actions as a means for seeking spiritual liberation.

Dr. Martin Luther King Jr. once was quoted as saying, "What does not destroy me makes me stronger."

"Know how sublime a thing it is to suffer and be strong."

Longfellow

How we endure when we are at our lowest mental state. It is difficult to carry on when grief over the loss of a loved one. When there's a very sick child with an incurable disease. There are many difficult moments that are in the heart spills over.

Coping with a marriage that has reached a dead end. It is sad to think when two people take their vows to love and cherish each other forever, find living another day together to be unbearable. One's thinking is confused concentrating on all the hateful acts instead of solving solutions. Such wounds always leave a scar.

A wise person once said that, "Tears are agony in solutions." There are times that shedding tears is good, rather than trying to keep it within.

When the Katrina disaster struck, so many lost homes with all possessions, little insurance to carry them through the horrific frightening times. Strength to rationalize, and find a reasonable explanation to the problems takes true courage, not to panic, to hang in there and think with calmness.

"Prayer is the wing wherewith the soul flies to heaven and meditation the eye wherein we see god."

Ambrose

Many a time through prayer, it lifts our spirit, and shines a light, giving us strength to find peace of mind to continue to forge ahead.

The truest courage is mixed with vigilance; concern which discriminating between courage, being wise and one being impulsive and foolish. This is not how you want your mind to work.

Thinking with a cool brain gets you working out the problem faster then with a hot mind. Being agitated gets you no where fast. Your mind is filled with fear, racing through a troubled rationalization. What all these problems bring on is stress.

It is said by psychologist, to feel and understand our stress early. How we are acting out our bad feelings, the sooner we check it in the bud, the better the results. Hold on there—slow down, gain some perspective. It helps to return to a better balanced mood—less stressed—happier! Smiling is a darn sight better looking than deep frown lines.

EVERYONE NEEDS A SMILE

"Housework will never kill you, but why take a chance?"

Phyllis Diller

I've said before, the only good thing about suffering is that each of us can feel what the other person is going through. Suffering is a lesson learned in compassion and courage.

We all have personal power to pull ourselves out of our problem through how we form tough, mental attitudes. To think tomorrow is a new day brings, to a more peaceful mind to make our days worthwhile. It helps how you live with aim of purpose, setting goals, being actively engaged, can truly change your mood for the better. Making you aware on the proper frame of mind will help to stay young while growing old.

Strike out two of the most harmful words to your mind:

"**Impossible!**" Makes you unsure.
"**Can't!**" Makes you defeated before you start.

I remind you again no one can be happy and healthy living for himself. Life owes us nothing. We owe it everything! We should live with loving life and having life, love back at us.

We humans are complicated beings. Suggestions in the book living life with thought and purpose, is not impossible to achieve. Living with others takes thought respect and flexibility for each of us have our own way of thinking and acting upon a situation.

So as long as we do not live in this world of only "me, myself" than one must firstly know, who we are so that we can better know, who the other person is. Fear, worry, are all part of the human psyche that we are constantly working to understand and overcome, which helps us keep our logic and handle the many daily challenges and keep us stress free.

We go from living in our parent's home, protected, emulating their values, with their many set of rules, and principles. Living as an adult on our own, sharing our life with another, again having to make more decisions under different circumstances. And once more as our daily life unfolds raising a family growing, having their own strong personalities. Life is constantly changing. We are subject to the natural ebb tides the flow of human emotions. There is a strong pull— rise and fall in everything. This is nature at work. We are a force of nature.

There are times when our bodies are down. Other times we are up. This is the cycle built within all of us. Recognizing when we have this low period it that too shall pass. It only remains if we let our thoughts pull us in the same direction. We have the choice how we want our life to be.

Nothing stays - it has to leave our thought process. You have an inner-voice telling us each moment how our thoughts should be. Distractions can be as simple as telemarketing phone calls when ready to sit down to your evening meal. Eliminate these distractions, and have your name removed on their list. It helps relieve stress. There's a solution to every problem.

Staying Young to 100 isn't impossible. Tom Lane, an American competitive swimmer at 103 is still alive doing his thing. To the Baby Boomers, some younger, some older - it seems a hundred years is much too long to think. One thing for sure, whatever age, keep your brain in shape keeping on top of events, keep in the present moment. Make every minute count. Don't take life for granted that you will remain healthy.

Moments like this are what we all need from time to time. It keeps us feeling alive and energized.

Kids aren't getting enough exercise, overweight, diabetes dangerously increasing. For one thing, parents have to make an exerted effort to change their life style if we want to see them grow mature and healthy.

Families that eat dinner together, lowers their stress. Studies have been made that there is less juvenile delinquency and obesity.

Kids go from school to their computers and sit for hours till supper time Mind gives us control. Your great tool is mind. Our success, happiness, our future are all determined in the mind. The ability to think is the real essence of human beings. Exchanging ideas stimulate the brain.

CHAPTER 46

Keys to Live By

"A sound head, an honest and humble spirit are best guides through time and eternity."

Anonymous

Keys to Live By:

1. **First knowing some of your strengths and weaknesses;**
2. **Working as hard as you can, to be the best at what you do;**
3. **To have the ability to smile and enjoy life;**
4. **Knowing to let go anger, hates, resentments;**
5. **Try to make each day a Masterpiece;**

People who live to 100 follow these rules, and understand their importance. Reflecting back in the 19th and 20th century, to those years when many of our grandparents first came to America, to a new country with little money. Not able to speak the language, no job— they had courage and hope. It took leaving what they had to venture so far away to start anew. It was a stressful time. Life had none of the comforts that we now have. People labored hard at long hours to earn a meager living. People looked old before their time. They died young.

All the mechanical speed saving gadgets, making the day go easier that we have weren't on the market. Air conditioning was unheard of. The simple electric fan was later made available. In the heat of summer, people living in the city in large tenement buildings suffered, and if possible slept outside on their fire escapes to catch a breeze.

Relaxing, enjoying some of life's simple pleasures were very few and far between. One didn't have many choices. Families and friends had fun picnicking in the parks. Playing games required very little money.

The head of the household, 90 percent was the man working outside the home. The young with the mother did piece work known as home industry, bringing in an additional small income to the household.

In the 21st century, we've come a long way making lives easier, healthier, longer lived with all the modern convinces at our finger tips. But are we wiser how to cope with less anxiety, less stress than our grandparent's who had so little? They looked to the future in a new wonderful land with positive feelings.

Researchers look at the human beings as a package, taking in biology, psychology, and culture. We should have less stress in our lives and the feeling of contentment should be uppermost.

What is the problem? There seems more than one. Stop and think with it all that makes living in the physical sense, we humans don't seem to be fulfilled emotionally enough. Can it be that we have lost sound reasoning? Our comfort zone is invaded like some thirsty beast craving, ever wanting, never satisfied—more stuff—more! Living many times beyond one's means. Adding more stress to our daily life.

Did you know that office workers are buying Silly Putty to knead away stress? During drive-time traffic report, the word "Road rage," is now in the dictionary.

While one sits in traffic it is a known fact that people are using the time making cell-phone calls or gulping down drive-thru food. Wow! That should tell you something what's happening to the human psyche. One needs a new mind set. Is it ever wonder that we are a society of stress and anxiety ridden people with all these modern "time-savers?" More and more stuff is sandwiched in a day. I can't help think — without considering one's priorities, one is left emotionally more frazzled, more stressed— feeling old and not complete.

We are our worse enemies. Taking on more and more, finding less and less time for self. One should decide what you will do and won't do. It takes knowing how to make decisions, and holding firm to priorities. If you take on extra projects at work, because you want the boss to recognize you're very capable, only adds to your stress level if you can't handle it—don't tax yourself.

Mind over matter, be aware how frequently you do things that you really don't want to do. Stop, don't respond with "yes." Think about your priorities. Soon others around in your household will get use to a "no," rather than a quick "yes," leaving you less stressed, finding time for self to enjoy more every day living. I ask, isn't this what we all want? I can't imagine anyone not wanting some time for self to relax. It boggles the mind just to think what is asked of one person in a day.

Put a halt and remind yourself what your needs are and stick to it. As was stated earlier, you are only one, and they are many hands. Be selfish, you will last longer, look better growing old. How's your mind working? Have you used sound reasoning yesterday—what about today?

Many can relate to male midlife crisis, a time of questioning values and goals. Menopause may affect a woman's perception and experience of the physical changes associated with change of life. Women more than men report going through stressful midlife "menopause" transition by age 50, according to a Cornell University study.

Man's midlife turmoil is more likely to be driven by work. Where as a woman's more often begins with family problems: difficulties with children, ill parents, divorce. Midlife is when long-buried desires resurface. You have to pause, and ask yourself what risks you need to take to honor the parts of yourself, you have been ignoring? What have you always longed to do and never have?

The more women have set something what they had always wanted to do were those, who weren't afraid to try anything new. Not all midlife changes that one wants to experience are big and dramatic. Some women discovered that they like to travel. Some took up signing up for various classes, one such as photography. Remember during restless, confused times strong feelings are apt to obscure good judgment.

During this mid-life period it is common that up until now everything you did is wrong is a common symptom. You might blame some of your unhappiness on you partner. Good support to successfully getting through a midlife time is where families can be a very helpful source of encouragement. Let them know what you are going through. They might see certain changes, which are puzzling to them. Hopefully they will be patient with understanding. Some of the support comes from outside the family, from people who are experiencing similar crises.

Many years ago, 12 women formed what they called the "Dream Salon" to talk about something they dreamed about doing, no matter how outlandish. These women in their 40's and 50's started businesses, earned degrees, thanks to this group. During this midlife crisis is the opportunity to support those who come after you. Pass on what you learned to younger associates, that the second half of your life is something to look forward to, not to fear. Keeping in shape both physically and mentally, to know that this too shall pass. That the emotional affects the physical, and the physical affects the emotional.

CHAPTER 47

Principles Staying Young

"Only as high as I reach can I grow; only as far as I seek can I go; only as deep as I look can I see; only as much as I dream can I be."

Karen Ravin

Marie Osmond made news once again when she decided to go on the television show, "Dancing with the Stars." She had been out of the lime light was busy being a mom. It showed determination as she never did dancing learning many new routines for this show. During all that practicing she lost 23 pounds. She mentioned from it all, she was rejuvenated and very happy.

Eight principles- to help you stay happy:

1. **Remember that the impact on "Attitude" how you look at things: is more important than failures, than circumstances, than what other people think or say or do.**
2. **Remember you have a "Choice"— every day.**
3. **Remember to take "time for self."**

4. Remember "Yesterday is Gone, Tomorrow starts new."
5. Remember "Mind over matter, Positive Thinking."
6. Remember you are a "Nurturing Being," give kind, loving service.
7. Remember to work toward "Goals and Dreams."
8. Remember to keep your "Priorities" in order.

Try to remember your priorities, goals, choices. Keep in mind that each one, including your attitude will keep you well balanced. Pay attention to your feelings. Observe your thinking. Don't let negative thoughts side track you from being happy —make each day a masterpiece!

Keep in mind the connection of those eight principles, which help to give more positive structure to your days. Having you think before you leap is going in a positive direction, with the mental dynamics of happiness.

All women have much in common—moms in the sandwich years living crazy multitasked lives. Everyone living in this 21st Century must learn not to sandwich doing so many tasks, so much in the course of a day, but pull back living less stressed out lives. There must be time for self!

Slowing down never hurt anyone. Don't clutter your day with a lot of detail. Spend some time by yourself. When you become more aware that you, me everyone, is expendable. Think about this it takes something from our importance. It makes your ego is slightly dented. Just be in a hospital for a few days and see how quickly you're replaced at work. The world goes on just the same with, or without all of us.

Remember the quote from Deepak Chopra when he said, "Does it ever occur to you that you can't lose anything, because you never had it in the first place? The only thing you've ever really had is yourself."

When you think of what he is saying... one thing is to know oneself is most important. Life owes us nothing, we owe it everything. Now is the only time that really exists. There is a wellspring of life within each of us. We must live each day to the fullest. If we know to do some of the right things, it will reward us with positive moments.

Everyone runs through a daily cycle of highs and lows. The unconscious mind has no definite time to solve problems. It works any time, it picks its own time and place. Studies by Dr. Nathaniel Kleitman, once associated with the University of Chicago, mentions that the mind is creative when we are on the high cycle, and sluggish when it is down. If you are a night person, your mind will be great in the evening to be creative.

Ernest Hemingway said he always started at the earliest part of the morning. He started to create at the first light. People have differences.

Yes, clear thinking is rare. We must be ready to sacrifice some of our own personality of thought as we face each new problem. Your thinking is part of your life's experience. The patterns in your brain are you own. Your opinion is the result of past experience.

Your past experiences may not always be consistent with those you have relationships both in the home and outside. Each of us carry, without realizing, a lot of poignant baggage around. If you have resolved within yourself certain issues, and a co-worker or companion hasn't, it takes patience solving mutual issues.

It is helpful to keep a daybook about feelings, moods, about priorities. It could be a guidepost to your life. If you can write something each day a little before you go to bed, it will give you insight how you better understand self and understand those at home and on the job. The written word is very powerful. It will become a reminder what is important, how wise you where that day with more positive action. You begin to see things— to sort out and have a better idea what is taking place daily. You will understand and live your life as you want.

The mind is capable of amazing changes. If you maintain a positive frame of mind, build a strong foundation, you will think differently and have fewer frustrations. Process your down moods and find alternatives creating a life you want. Never settle for "can't." Remember "try" opens closed doors, introduces you to living life happier, and stay young while growing old.

Ask yourself how many roses you deserve. One? five?

"Because—I realize that my attitude keeps me on the right path, because—I am successful in my relationships at home at work, because—I am kind knowing each of us are fighting a hard battle."

It was once said that you can make more friends in a month by being interested in them, than in ten years by trying to get them interested in you.

STAY YOUNG TO 100

When I was a Commissioner for the Rockford Park District, I met hundreds, who gave so much of their time on the job. They knew me by name and it became a mutual caring society. Many appreciated the effort I personally gave attention to, and my sincere services. In the six years, I never forgot to pay a compliment. Now no longer on the job, when we happen to meet on the street, they still remember me by name, and some with a warm hug.

CHAPTER 48

It's all In the Journey

"To know how to grow old is the master-work of wisdom, in the art of living difficult."

Anonymous

From time to time, I like to concentrate on what's not wrong with human beings and more on developing what is right, so we will gain and create fulfillment. Knowing that change is difficult, and to understand self isn't always easy. It takes time to develop, let alone understand who we are or will be. "It is all in the journey."

Statistics from the U.S. Census Bureau of 2002, taken the number of Centenarians in 2010 the year before the Baby Boomers start turning 65, to be 129,000. Will you be one of them? It is predicted that there may be as many as 2,500,000 persons 100+. Stay with that thought.

It was said that the happiest people are those who come nearest to living their dreams. A happy life is active with friends and family. Being courageous, going out on that limb, tasting the fruit, having the tenacity to work making some dreams a reality. It is the experience that fulfills us. So live life, have the experience of interesting people, who keep you alive and interesting.

To make a change living to a healthy 100 is the key for having maturity. Too often we are stuck emotionally. Becoming what we are is sometimes a long journey. But it is in the journey we learn who we are, and can understand better who that other person is. Each with their hopes and dreams and like us—fears.

If one keeps mind over matter where you want to be, it can make one's dream not too far off in the distance. It is the power within you and how daily you focus on where you're going. Talk to yourself, be reinforced, and hear your positive feedback.

Remember that word "Should?" I mentioned it in the very early chapter when I lost my son and was having so many emotional problems. I focused on that word and it gave me food for thought and helped change the actions of my daily life. "I should— stop taking tranquilizers! I should— stop drinking—I should begin to start living with a purpose!"

Sometimes we all need to stop and say thanks to something we are grateful for. It doesn't need to be something large. It can be as small as a neighbor bringing in a plate of homemade cookies this New Year's Day, in exchange for a kindness you long forgot. It brought a smile and warmed your heart. Since Sam died, there have been lonely moments. Receiving that neighbor's small token made me realize that she appreciated me and had my interest in mind.

With everyone rushing round in this fast paced world, one has to be reminded about gratitude and how the action of doing or giving can have such a wonderful impact, both on the giver and receiver. With every passing day try and see that you have done something nice for others, especially those who cannot do for themselves. When writing in your daybook, mention what you feel thankful for. Send a note to anyone who effects your life positively. E-mail is so, but a personal hand written note is more meaningful.

Good feelings release dopamine, the chemical in the brain associated with happiness. Dopamine releases in that part of the brain that stimulates logic and reason. By keeping note of these feelings and what brought it on, you will appreciate its impact on you and help you be more aware what went right this day, rather than what went wrong. Positive input over and over again, has many inner spiritual rewards.

Human beings constantly surprise me with the will and strength of mind to achieve their goal. I witnessed several Olympic athletics practicing, which involve hours of intensive, strenuous gymnastic activities. It almost took my breath away just watching the tremendous feats of energy explode on the gym floor, with their high leaps in the air, tumbling, cart-wheels, fancy flip-over steps on a narrow four inch plank high off the ground. Their performance was more natural to monkeys than man.

Occasionally I would watch the fights on television with my husband. It amazed me how much punishment the human body can take. But the determination to win is more surprising, when you see the brutal beating that one endures. In spite how many times the fellow was knocked down, his determination, his super will power, gave him the mind to keep going. He managed with his last bit of strength to pull himself up and land the winning punch. It isn't how many times one falls, but to have the grit to get back up, that's the important thing.

President Calvin Coolidge coined the slogan "press on," in his written saying, he goes on—"determination and persistence alone are invincible, has solved and always will solve the problems of the human race." And so human nature has many parallel defining moments throughout one's life. To find strength of purpose, not to yield defeat and to get back up and start over—one is a winner. I had several defining moments in my life. With determination and persistence it made me a stronger person. I was able to pull myself up and be a part of the human race once again.

There isn't one human being on this planet who hasn't had some daily problems. Some face their problems decisively, while others it is an effort. Having creative power, figuring how to get out of a bad situation takes mental attitude—the ability to visualize what one desires to attain despite failure. Your subconscious mind is constantly at work. If you can maintain some optimism you will gain confidence, pushing aside fear and worry along with your down mood. Slowly you will start seeing beyond your troubles. When you are happy, you are able to think better. When you are more positive, good things happen to you. Researchers found that people who focus on what they are thankful for are more buoyant, tough and resistant.

Expressing feelings in words short-circuits the body's reaction by preventing stress hormones from being released. So if you are troubled it helps sometimes to communicate with someone near to you, a relative a friend. It lowers your stress level. What you put forth, making your days more fulfilling, is an everyday challenge. Every moment of each day you have to draw upon, making right decisions for self. Life is constantly changing, making another decision, making adjustments. Grappling, reaching for more understanding of self and hoping for others.

CHAPTER 49

Let Go Of It

"Things without remedy should be without regard; what is done is done."

Shakespeare

Get on with your life. This is easier said than we can sometimes do. It is hard to let go and free the mind when a dear one has died, when a relationship went bad, when many incidents are still hurtful years later. As you keep repeating in your head the same lament which slowly takes over your life, leaving no room for enjoying your days and even disrupting your sleep.

There is a biological reason for the power that holds onto your thoughts. The human brain has a special biochemical "circuitry transmission" for survival. It is what tells you to eat when hungry. It is a circuit in the brain that one can be hooked by nicotine and alcohol. It is also patterns or rituals that sometimes referred to as addictions.

We have ceremonies for various things— birthdays, marriage, death. These are the rituals which play an important role in life's passages. These rituals have the power of marking time and moving us from one stage to another, an intermission in time in our lives. It helps broadens our perspective on our behavior, accepting the realities that each face. We cannot and should not run from it.

Some of us are more fragile while others seem to be able to set aside like Grandma Moses, discarding the bad times. There are a few visible signs that should make you aware having this form of addiction:

*If still, after a year or so... you are mourning over your deceased....

*If still, not over a breakup of a relationship....

*If still, friends and family haven't the importance they once had....

*If still, having your down mood and your job is in jeopardy....

Recognize that you are addicted to being depressed and should realize it can be serious and to express these continued feelings to someone. A physiologist is good to talk to.

You can speak your thoughts freely out loud. Bottled up feelings will not free you from painful memories. By expressing yourself honestly it will help letting go. A very close friend that you respect can help sometimes to talk over feelings.

Personal relationships...work satisfaction...spiritual growth... social harmony are all linked to mind and body very intimately. Do not stay closed off away from family.

Every day have a plan of meeting a friend or two and start getting back to activities that you once enjoyed. Do something that marks a new beginning of letting go. Life must not be lived daily in mental pain. One must do some soul searching and realize this form of addiction of mental self punishment is very harmful. Daily reliving painful memories is not rational.

Taking proper steps having a conscious appreciation what is around you, more positive thoughts "Letting Go!" will generate moving you forward for a healthier, happier existence.

Deepak Chopra said, "The way you experience the world depends just as much, or more on the quality of your perceptions as it does on whatever is being perceived. If you are experiencing a sense of balance, creatively and inner fulfillment, this is what you will find all around you."

I like to call an "inner voice" that speaks to us when we're about to do something we shouldn't do, or it helps like radar to the brain. It speaks telling us oncoming trouble. This voice resounding in your head cautions us for some possibility not realized. That inner voice is "you!" Paying attention it helps making good and bad decisions.

Recently in the evening, coming home from a late meeting I realized I didn't have any milk for breakfast. Pulling into the parking lot of the grocery store it seemed overly dark. I had a strange feeling, and thought instead of taking my purse I would take five dollars, nothing more, and placed my purse under the seat.

Stepping out of the car, a fellow came out of nowhere, approached me. He said, "Lady you're getting a flat on your rear tire, I can fix it." And with that he shoved me back against the car and mumbled "give me your purse!" Surprised and scared, all I could say was, "here, this is all I have!" Holding out my hand with the five dollars, he snatched it and ran.

I stood for a moment, trembling, then went into the store to report the incident. The police were notified and asked for a description. When I returned home I turned on my television and there appeared a photograph of the same man that approached me—they had just caught him.

So whatever my inner-voice like some radar was sending signals out to me, that evening, I was very happy that I listened and hide my purse, so all he got was a five dollar bill. It could have been worse.

I couldn't help thinking of my friend Betty, who was attacked walking in the park and remembered what my feelings were. It was that same inner-voice that told me what she was about to do wasn't safe. I call it intuition, both are one of the same, the mind speaking to us, forewarning, which can help safe guard against oncoming trouble.

In the long run we can't get away with anything in life that we don't pay a price for— there's payback. What goes around comes around.

Something like a bad experience takes moments to collect ones self and begin focusing on something, to rest the mind filled with the moment. Relax, count your blessings, it could have been worse. Your mind and your body are the most valuable possession. To be able to greet another day is how you should think.

One's subconscious mind, using mental awareness automatically comes out a winner. It's important how we think. Examine your thoughts. Are your thought patterns like your parents? Do you see yourself yelling at your kids the same way you were constantly put down?

These patterns that stick in one's brain are not mental awareness. Reflect on becoming aware by decision not to continue in the same patterns that you dislike from others. Realize that whatever you think and believe becomes so. You inherited the color of your skin, your eyes, but you are emotionally marked by your home environment, the people from so early on that you have no recollection.

One thing that is upper most important is when you understand "self," you best understand others.

"Remember that you are a child of the universe unfolding as it should. Therefore, be at peace with god, whatever you conceive him to be, and whatever your labors and aspirations, in this noisy confusion of life, keep peace with your soul...with all its sham, drudgery and broken dreams, it is still a beautiful world. Be careful... strive to be happy."

Desiderata

A portion from: Found in Old Saint Paul's Church Baltimore, Date 1692

Dear Reader,

I hope my book illuminates and gives light to your days. Congratulate yourself for you are on your way understanding self with more positive thoughts, growing more confident, changing old behaviors, recognizing your potential, and how special you are.

You are the most important person in your life. Treat yourself with tender loving care. Be your own best friend. Embrace all the goodness that you can and focus on living life fuller, with less fears, less doubts, less stress.

Take into account that one's positive attitude boosts our spirit against problems, and opens the soul to simple pleasures, extends our optimism, and makes our life lived well, happy, healthy and wise.

Learn by heart the 10 life lessons and use them in your relationships, with family, and work. Remember that life is a journey. We learn by our mistakes, and grow stronger by overcoming them. After we all improve little bit by little bit, step by step and day by day.

Make the rest of your life, the best of your life

RESOURCES

Exercise, Eat, Clean Diet Workout
Tosca Reno

Let Me Remember
Iyanka Vanzant

Living Younger
Dr. Evan Kligman

Organic Food Shoppers Guide
Jeff Cox

Researcher study of Centenarian
Dan Buettneer 2008

Smart Money Decisions
Max Bazerman PHD 2002

The Relaxation Response
Herbert Benson

The Success Principles
Jack Canfields Books

Wisdom and Healing
Deepak Chopra
Page-A-Day-Calendar

Happy For No Reason
Marci Shimoff & Carol Kline
Free Press 2008

Change Your Brain Change Your Life
Three Rivers Press NY, NY 2007

The Four Noble Truths
Dalai Lama
Harper Collins NY 2004

Sierra Club Magazine
Healthy Life 2008

NOTES